In Due Season

PRAYER
FOR AUTUMN,
ADVENT, CHRISTMAS
AND WINTER
FEASTDAYS

Ken Phillips

*For Bill my gratitude for a season of shared prayer.
Ken Phillips*

TWENTY THIRD 23rd PUBLICATIONS
www.23rdpublications.com

DEDICATED TO MY FRIEND,
OCCASIONAL MUSE, AND CHALLENGER
SISTER PATRICIA SCHNAPP, RSM
WHO HOUNDED ME FROM MY
MID-TWENTIES TO GET PUBLISHED.

"Without a Vision, the people perish..."

TWENTY-THIRD PUBLICATIONS
1 Montauk Avenue, Suite 200, New London, CT 06320
(860) 437-3012 » (800) 321-0411 » www.23rdpublications.com

© Copyright 2014 Ken Phillips. All rights reserved.
No part of this publication may be reproduced in any manner without prior written permission of the publisher. Write to the Permissions Editor.

ISBN: 978-1-62785-026-1
Library of Congress Catalog Card Number: 2014940878
Printed in the U.S.A.

Contents

Foreword
PAGE vii

Part I
At the Old New Year
PAGE 1

Part II
The Winter Passage
PAGE 37

Part III
Winter into Spring
PAGE 97

Acknowledgments

Some time ago, I came to the earth-shattering realization that none of us gets anywhere, particularly anywhere of consequence, by ourselves. I think it may only be the hubris-ridden who think otherwise. Believing that this book is a very special "somewhere" in my life, I wish to publically thank some of the people who helped me get to this particular place.

I wish to thank the gracious staff of Twenty-Third Publications who encouraged this book into existence, particularly in an age when books are on the endangered species list. I suspect that there are possibly people who will derive great meaning from reading prayers from electronic screens in their individual devotions, but, as the Great Master paintings of the Virgin at the Annunciation intimate, we don't have lots of (say) pictorial evidence that reminds us that the Divine enters the everyday very readily without a book at hand. So thanks to all people who craft books into being, but especially Therese Ratliff, Dan Connors, Jeff McCall, Dan Smart, and Kerry Moriarty.

Second, I wish to thank a few of the communities that have encouraged my prayer/poem writing over the years. Chiefly, Regis University in Denver, Colorado, through its encouragement of ecumenical and interfaith shared prayer, and also St. Barnabas Episcopal Church, Berkeley Community United Church of Christ, and North Highland Presbyterian Church, all also of Denver, Colorado. Each time I prepare the written word for a new community, I grow in understanding of both how important and how problematic language can be. Words are the doors by which we keep people out and bring people in, either consciously or unconsciously.

I am grateful for every conference, every liturgical, musical, or ministerial gathering for which I have had the pleasure of writing original material. Groups large and small reminded me of the power of repeated speech, speech with marked rhythms and sounds, and words that invited imagination to balance the rigors of rubric.

Each time I accomplish any creative goal, I am forced to realize that the seeds of my creative life were planted in my unlikely ground by nuns. Oh the nuns! Heavens that the nuns of old may have a renaissance, with their fire, their strength, their words of encouragement (and insistence), and, especially, their stunning ability to produce something out of nearly nothing. So, wherever ye may be, Sister Rose Henrice, Sister Catherine George, Sisters Angela Marie, Judine, Pauline, Geraldine, Celeste, Paulette, Joyce, and Patricia—thanks! But most crucial thanks to Rose Gilbert La Bonty, OP, who said "Be All You Can Be" before the Army did.

Finally, to the wondrous Kathy Hendricks, who created a bridge where once there was none, thank you for encouragement, deadlines, and redlines, and the magical power of simple belief. You make things happen. Can you blame me for thinking you a creature of another realm?

Ken Phillips
MAY 2014
DENVER, COLORADO

Foreword

The landscape of prayer is a rich and varied terrain, ranging from the heartfelt "oh, God!" in a moment of shock to the more elaborate liturgical ceremonies in which we engage with our diverse faith communities. Different events lead us to different stances and attitudes of prayer. Whether in celebrations of the Lord's Supper or candlelit vigils on street corners, our bodies, brains, and souls are engaged according to where and how we are invited to address "the Great Other." Our needs, our joys, the varied mysteries of our lives are served by speech, sound, and gesture that can be spontaneous or formal. Most folks recognize that prayer is sometimes most appropriate as a solitary experience; at other times, the presence of a community is necessary to match the joy or the grief that compel us to give voice to a special inner language. And, of course, the impact of seasons and times, festivals and calendars makes itself known in how we use language, arrange our spaces, and lift up our hearts to the One Who Knows Us Best.

In Due Season is a volume of various kinds of prayers. Some are constructed as personal, more poetic, meditations—pieces that are meant, like most poetry, to be digested, perhaps bits at a time, or to be bathed in, in their sounds and senses, in a whole. Some are fitting as meditations for private reading or for interpretive reading as parts of prayer services. Others of these prayers are meant for communal gatherings, retreats, alternative prayer gatherings, and so forth. Intended for lay leadership and communal participation, these prayers are fitting around a single expanded table, in the home, around campfires, before or after meetings, or wherever groups of people want to give special expression to their faith identity, their spiritual journeys, their varied searches for the Divine, so often found in their midst.

The language is ritual language. It is poetic, inviting us to consider the Holy through the images of everyday life as well as through the images of our faith stories. The lines flow sometimes like natural speech and sometimes like music, engaging the repeated rhythms found in hymns or songs. They can be read spontaneously out loud—or interpreted vocally by someone who cares to uncover their poetic devices with some study or practice—like a good Pauline letter. They can be contemplated quietly, unpacked in private mediation or prayer. They can accompany a passage of a retreat or give voice to a community gathered in a liturgical season.

There are seasonal table prayers, which work well before a community meal and allow for a different form of the breaking of bread and the sharing of the fruit of the vine. There are communal prayers for festivals and saints days. There are litanies and prayers of the people for various occasions, most of which can be interwoven in established liturgies or used independently.

This volume takes its lead from the roots of a late Fall "New Year" planted long ago in the Celtic Year. At Samhain (end of harvest, beginning of the darker part of the year), the separating of the worlds grew thin, and movement from the world of the living to the world of the other-life allowed translation of beings not possible at other times of the year. This possibility of the sight of other things is a good lens for considering ritual behavior and meditational practice. It gives us ways of opening up to worlds of spirit that are sometimes far from us in our workaday existences, scribed as they are by time frames that sometimes make us blind to a larger reality. We need to step outside of "our time" upon occasion so that we might understand our time more fully.

From the fall triduum (days of the dead), the prayers move through fall to harvest time and Thanksgiving. Then, as winter commences, we pass through the beginning of the Church year in the season of Advent/Christmas/Yuletide, the calendar New Year, Epiphany, Valentine's Day, and on toward Mardi Gras and the conclusion of the carnival season that began at Epiphany. The book offers different perspectives on the feasts that we know well, or about which we may have forgotten. Each piece is an invitation to take a slightly different look at the feasts and festivals that enrich our lives and reflect on what our lives are already about.

The pieces can be used for individual reflection within the book. Small communities may consider multiple volumes as additional aids for communal prayer, and pieces can be reproduced for larger groups, acknowledging author, book title, copyright, and publisher information.

Part I

AT THE OLD NEW YEAR

In October

A Service of Prayer Near the Feast of Guardian Angels

APPLICATION

The feast of Michaelmas, or the feast of Michael and the Archangels, or All Angels, has been observed on September 29. In the Roman Calendar, October 2 (in some places the first Sunday of September) is the feast of Guardian Angels. Whichever the date, the Angels are remembered in near conjunction with the fall equinox and the end of the agrarian year.

SET UP

This can be prayed by a group gathered around a single (expanded) table or in a circle. Icons or paintings of angels can be within the space along with a variety of candles. All have a copy of the text. Have some sort of device for playing recorded music. Where resources and talent exist, live harp music would be great.

A deck of "Angel Cards" (Compassion, Strength, Patience, Wisdom, Attentiveness, Courage, etc.) can be used at the end of the prayers of petition. These cards are available commercially or can be made for the prayer.

The prayer can be read antiphonally on two sides, or other designations can be made. The parts in bold are read by all.

CALL TO PRAYER

The prayer can begin with some sort of call to mindfulness (quiet, intentional breathing) and then move into instrumental music and the lighting of the candles (perhaps some incense) around the images/icons. A leader begins the prayer when all are ready.

OPTIONAL READING/ SHARING ABOUT ANGELS

e.g.: Psalm 34, Psalm 91, Colossians 1:16, other sources

ANGEL ANTIPHONAL INVOCATION

A: Angels of God,
Come to our aid!
B: Agents of Grace,
Make haste to help us!

**Lights born of Light,
When Night gathers 'round.
Come and be with us!
Stand by our side.**

A: You winged ministers
Who do God's will,
B: Shield us and guard us;
protect us still.

**Timeless in beauty,
Ageless and strong,
In love attend us,
Guide us from wrong.**

A: Voice of the Holy,
B: Music of Heaven,

**Aid our prayer.
Join us in song.**

A: Speak to us. Help us.
In this place, Mystery is waiting.
B: Speak to us. Help us.
Around this place,
Shadows are growing.

Speak to us. Help us.
Let no mortal shake us;
Let no dark overpower.
Open a doorway for our
understanding.
At this threshold,
in this hour,
Be our guardians
and show us the way.

SIMPLE PRAYERS OF THE PEOPLE

(Where do you need guidance, protection, aid, special companionship?)

(At the end of the prayer, participants draw an "Angel Card" with an option for sharing what they have drawn and its significance for them, if any.)

A MUSIC MEDITATION

- *Sarah McLachlan's "Angel"*
- *Jane Siberry's "Calling All Angels"*
- *The Guardian Angel Prayer from Humperdinck's opera "Hansel and Gretel"*
- *"Mad About Angels" CD Collection. Deutsche Grampahone.*

A CLOSING PRAYER

O Presence, source of light,
enduring love, power
beyond my own,

O Touch of the Divine,
minister of the Eternal,
Shield of Grace,
Understanding beyond my own,

Enfold me
with wings to protect.

Surround me
with light that makes
clear the way.

Guide me
with words speaking
to my heart.

Instruct me
with knowledge for my spirit.

Counsel me
with wisdom for my soul.

Accompany me
in times of doubt.

Give me utterance
in times of joy.

Give me strength
in seasons of weakness.

Give me courage
in moments of fear.

Abide with me and speak to my true and best self, that I may journey to my everlasting Home with humility, assurance, and love that makes itself known in true words and loving works.

AMEN.

■ ■ ■

At the Old New Year

MEDITATION

Seasons of Change: Autumn

The day has moved from
silent grey and fog
into the wild embrace of wind
that strips those stubborn oaks
of their tan-gold, leathery leaves.
They held on for so long.
They are the last
    of their kind to go.

The brief gold of late afternoon
has melted into a strange
middling space
where every breath
ushers in a change.
Now
everything is yielding to
the advancing cold
that will certainly creep in
in the hours of evening
while I am sleeping.

All this
my single window has
framed for me
in the brief span of hours
of this autumn day.
Dark falls even earlier now;
my eyes, my skin,
my taste can tell.
I am at the still point
of the change,
and I feel You in it.

Then hold me, God,
in this present stillness.
hold me from the rush within.

Settle me, O God,
in this present stillness.
Settle me from the rush
    without—
the wind-stripped trees,
the urgent endings,
the furious undoing
    of everything.

Calm me, O God,
in this present stillness
where I may perceive
Your whisper
in my soul,
even as everything changes.

Keep me, O God,
in this present stillness.
Let me find You in my breath.

One breath.

A deeper breath.

Another breath that slows me.

My mind.

My anxious clutching of
a controlled exterior
that also is being
stripped away,
as it must.

I am surrendering
even as the oak.

Love me, God,
in this present stillness
where I am resting in You,
even as everything falls,
as it must,
to earth.

I bless You, O God,
for this present stillness
where my spirit finds its home
that is only a reflection
of the Home I have
in You.
Here
in this present stillness
my closed eyes,
my sweatered skin,
my quieted tongue,
I can tell:

You are here.

Guide me, God,
from this present stillness
and bring me to You,
waiting,
working,
in my world.

Bring me back, O God,
to this present stillness,
that I may hold
a small part of You
in my heart
in the midst of other changes.

AMEN.

FOR WRITTEN OR SHARED REFLECTION

- In what season do I find myself these days?

- What are the outer manifestations of that season?

- What are the inner movements or signs of that season?

- What are the changes I feel happening in me? Within the circles of my life?

- Have I been here before?

The Autumn Triduum

It was only a few years ago that I first heard of the concept of a three-day (triduum) celebration in the fall that balanced the energy of the spring Holy Week Triduum. Though perhaps minor in stature compared to the Holy Thursday/Good Friday/Holy Saturday assemblage in the Church, the autumn triduum (All Hallows/All Saints/All Souls) carries much popular and multicultural weight. Living in a culture shaped by Mexican/South American influences, it's hard to escape the popular embrace of celebrations that take on the reality of human frailty and death, and the hope in the transcendence of the soul.

All Hallows' Eve (October 31, Halloween) has strong Celtic roots and reminds us that there is a realm of existence beyond our daily struggles, tedium, and triumphs. The world of retail reminds us that Halloween's significance has grown expansively in energy over the years, and it rivals even the Christmas season for purchases of decorations, clothing, and food. These prayers are one opportunity to claim its spiritual dimension.

All Saints' Day, the second of the fall triduum observances (November 1), was quite an event when I was growing up in Catholic schools. Dressing up as saints was meant, I think, to rival more ghoulish behaviors of Halloween, and the pageants and music were intended to give us something to contemplate besides the sugary loot we gathered on the last night of October. Though it did little to counter the obsession with trick or treating, it did seem to connect us to the belief that we were very much connected to these saints (the stories of whose martyrdoms were often far more grim and bloody than anything Hollywood could concoct). The concept of the "Mystical Body" in which all the living and the dead are connected in Christ has power in many ways and merits more contemplation and celebration than I think it may get traditionally.

The final part of the fall triduum, the feast of All Souls (November 2) is one that is gaining in popularity and awareness, again, in large part due to the influence of Hispanic culture in America. Both the feast and the time of year invite remembrance of those passed, and the customs and practices support a domestic spirituality that is vibrant, memorable, and exciting.

The following pieces are applicable to group or private settings and allow for various applications and inventions.

MEDITATION

At All Hallows' Eve

The tall priest
with grey hair
and eyes like
light through ice
spoke
in just
more than a whispered voice
that carried,
barely,
over candle tops
glowing gold in
    November half-light:

Of this season
when sun grows shy
and night creeps greedily
over its boundaries,
the Ancients said
that the veil
between our world
and the world of those
dead and
gone
grows thin,
so thin,
that they,
who are
the food of grief,
may slip
into our waking days
and we,
who are
the grieving,
may slip
into their long sleep
before our time.
And so,
our brave and nameless
ancestors
lit small lights
against the
cavernous dark,
to guide spirits
to hurried
memorial feasts,
and then back
to the gates
of the land
of their shadowy belonging,
ghost guts filled with
remembrance
and sips
of whiskey…

And as his words
evaporated
in the holy quiet,
I wondered
if those I lost to
time,
gunshot,
weak hearts,
and
failing lungs
were inching
near me,
full of secrets,
hungry for
sweet bread
and
living breath.

∎∎∎

An Autumn Table Prayer

For All Hallows' Eve

APPLICATION

A gathering on All Hallows' Eve, especially as an alternative to more popular secular (and sugar-laden) practices. Works well for an alternative Sabbath gathering, parish meeting, family gathering, retreat, ecumenical gathering of several communities, etc. This prayer form lends itself to a potluck and is great for a gathering where people are looking for a spiritual dimension to this popular celebration. (If the demands of observing Halloween itself in its traditional way are too great, consider this for an "Eve of the Eve" event.)

SET UP

This is prayed by a group gathered around a single (expanded) table, or at a series of tables. Tables can be set as simply or as elaborately as resources allow. Candlelight and tablecloths are conducive to the sense of a ceremonial meal. Pumpkins, gourds, apples, or fall leaves make for an easy environment to create.

At the table, all have a copy of the text and a glass. The fruit of the vine (wine or juice) is distributed to each person's glass at the table. A loaf of bread for breaking is in readiness at a leader's place, or loaves of bread can be present at each table.

Individuals read the numbered portions (this can be designated in advance or done at table, spontaneously). All read the parts in bold.

CALL TO PRAYER

The meal begins with an indication of the nature of the prayer, a touch of history, and some sort of call to mindfulness (quiet, intentional breathing or meditational music or a song). A designated leader lights a candle and begins the prayer when all are ready.

1) The Earth is rolling always onward.
   And the seasons are shifting.

Summer's work is coming to its end.
   We are surrounded by her fullness.

We have bread again, and wine.
   **And we are here to give thanks
   and to remember.**

---

2) O God of the Universe, once again the turning seasons show Your handiwork. Nature displays Your glory and reveals a wisdom we cannot deny.
   **The shortening of the days
   and the lingering night
   remind us of our own
   brief days upon the earth.**

---

3) And though marred by human toil, the beauty of the changing planet still speaks to us, if we are open.
   **We live our own seasons.
   We rise and fall. We bloom and bear fruit
   and return to the dust from
       which we are made.**

---

4) We learn from the changing seasons that all things come to an end.
   **And from those same seasons
       we know that new life
   springs up in the fullness of time.**

---

5) In the colors that amaze us, in the changes of land and sky and tree and field,
   **there is change and transformation,
   there is mystery unfolding,
   and glory, and beauty beyond
   our powers of speech or song.**

6) In the movement of the sun, we behold the precious light and the necessary dark.
> **Truly, Your Holy Wisdom is
> knit up in the fabric of everything
> that is around us.**

7) And now on this Eve of All Hallows, we recall those who have lived with us,
> **Those who have broken bread with us
> on the journey,**

Those who have shared wine and the fruit of their wisdom,
> **Those who have blessed us with their love,
> their struggles,
> their gifts of laughter, strength, and joy.**

8) We are filled with gratitude for the people who matter, for the gifts of this season, and for all that You give to us. So we praise You, Our Beloved, and together we proclaim:
> **The earth is Yours, O God,
> and all that is within her.
> She is the gift of Your hands.
> We taste her and learn from her,
> from the dance of her birth, her life,
> her dying, to her being born again.**

9) We are filled with gratitude for our ancestors, near and far-flung in time. Those known and unknown, those who are tied to us by blood, by lineage, by land, by tongue, by story, and by faith.
> **The people of earth are Yours, O God, and all
> that makes them, great or humble.
> They are the gift of Your hands.
> We sense them and learn from them,
> from the struggle of their births, their lives,
> their many dyings, to the stories of them
> making them born again.**

(We lift the bread for blessing.)

Blessed are You, Holy God of the Universe, for You give us bread to eat, formed from the grain that falls to the ground, that dies and springs forth again, fashioned into one loaf, broken and shared, that many may be fed together.
> **May it be our nourishment
> for the journey we make together,
> and a daily reminder of Your providence.**

(We break the bread and pass it round the table and eat a portion of it. When all have tasted, we continue.)

(We lift the fruit of the vine for blessing.)

Blessed are You, Holy God of the Universe, for You give us the fruit of the vine to drink. Crushed from many grapes, brought together to be poured out that many may be refreshed together.
> **May it be joy and grace
> for the journey we make together,
> and a reminder of the richness of Life.**

(We take a sip of the fruit of the vine together. When all have tasted, we continue.)

10) Blessed are You, Lord God of the Universe; in Your love, You give us people to cherish, bread to eat, and the fruit of the vine to drink that we may be sustained and renewed on the journey we make together.
> **May our remembrance make us loving.
> May grain keep us strong. May the fruit
> of the vine make us joyful. May all gifts in
> every season draw us closer to You, O Maker
> of our Precious Planet Home, Father and
> Mother of us all.
> Amen.**

∎ ∎ ∎

A Service of Scripture and Prayer

On the Feast of All Saints

APPLICATION

The feast of All Saints (all Hallows, Hallowmas), is observed in some form by most Christian churches. Its November 1 date has its foundation in a declaration by Pope Gregory III (731-741) requiring the recollection "of the holy apostles and of all saints, martyrs, and confessors, of all the just made perfect who are at rest throughout the world." There are variations among the Christian churches, and in different countries, as to how the feast is celebrated. Generally, it remembers those who lived some heightened model of the faith but also, in some cases, including the faithful departed from local church communities.

APPLICATION

Any form of personal, familial, or communal prayer on November 1. The prayer could be enhanced with a book of the lives of the saints (How much do you know about the saint you were named for?) and perhaps a list of people from families, communities, and churches who have died within the last year.

SET UP

This can be prayed in almost any setting; icons or images of saints can be useful, as can photographs of those who have died in your community. Candles (especially the paschal candle) can be useful in enhancing the environment. Bread and fruit of the vine are prepared for the *Agape*.

A musical setting of the litany of the saints is useful. Songs may be inserted in different parts of the prayer.

CALL TO PRAYER

The history of the feast can be shared. Call to mind our connection to those who have come before us in faith, their modeling of holiness for us, their examples of compassion, wisdom, prayerfulness, etc., that have helped to transform the Church, our lives, and our world. Begin with a call to be mindful of our connection in the Mystical Body of Christ, and move into the prayer when all are ready.

WELCOME

LEADER: Welcome to this holy place! Welcome to you, saints and sinners all! You who hunger for the face of God, you who strive for holiness and for wholeness, you who await the fullness of God's reign: you are all welcome here.

> **ALL: Alleluia! We have come to gather in the Spirit of the One who calls us as we praise Christ, who is our light and the joy of our salvation.**

LEADER: My friends, in our prayer today, we celebrate the body of Christ, which spans over time and space and reaches beyond even the shores of death. We recall in our prayer the holy women and men who have shaped this community, the Church, and our selves by their witness to Christ.

Let us begin by opening our minds, hearts, and imaginations to the words of Scripture.

A READING

Revelation 7:9–17

A reading from the Book of Revelation.

After this I, John, looked, and there was a great multitude that no one could count, from every nation, from all tribes and peoples and languages, standing before the throne and before the Lamb, robed in white, with palm branches in their hands. They cried out in a loud voice, saying, "Salvation belongs to our God who is seated on the throne, and to the Lamb!" And all the angels stood around the throne and around the elders and the four living creatures, and they fell on their faces before the throne and worshiped God, singing, "Amen! Blessing and glory and wisdom and thanksgiving and honor and power and might be to our God forever and ever! Amen."

Then one of the elders addressed me, saying, "Who are these, robed in white, and where have they come from?" I said to him, "Sir, you are the one that knows." Then he said to me, "These are they who have come out of the great ordeal; they have washed their robes and made them white in the blood of the Lamb. For this reason they are before the throne of God, and worship him day and night within his temple, and the one who is seated on the throne will shelter them. They will hunger no more, and thirst no more; the sun will not strike them, nor any scorching heat; for the Lamb at the center of the throne will be their shepherd, and he will guide them to springs of the water of life, and God will wipe away every tear from their eyes."

Hear what the Spirit is saying to all the Church.

Thanks be to God.

A RESPONSE

A Litany of the Holy Ones

(Modeled on a litany found in St. Augustine's Prayer Book. Another spoken or sung litany may be used.)

O Gracious God,
Creator of all that is,
℟. **We bless You
and give praise.**

O Loving Christ,
Son of Heaven and Earth, ℟.

O Holy Spirit,
Transforming Breath of God, ℟.

O Holy Trinity,
Mysterious, Ineffable God, ℟.

Miriam of Nazareth,
Mother of Jesus,
℟. **We remember
and give thanks.**

Michael the Archangel, ℟.

All holy Angels
and Archangels, ℟.

All Orders of Blessed Spirits, ℟.

Ancestors Abraham, Isaac,
and Jacob, ℟.

Faithful Moses, Miriam,
and Aaron, ℟.

Gracious and loving Ruth and
Naomi, ℟.

Holy Servants David, Samuel,
and Elijah, ℟.

Trusting Zachariah and
Elizabeth, ℟.

Prayerful Joachim and Anne, ℟.

John the Baptist,
messenger of God, ℟.

Joseph, Dreamer
and Protector, ℟.

All wise Patriarchs
and Prophets, ℟.

Blustering Peter
and Brave Paul, ℟.

At the Old New Year

Apostles Andrew, James, and John, ℟.

Evangelists Matthew, Mark, and Luke, ℟.

Beloved Mary of Magdala, ℟.

All first followers and proclaimers of Jesus, ℟.

Stephen, Ignatius of Antioch, and Polycarp, ℟.

Alban, Perpetua, and Felicity, ℟.

All you Faithful Martyrs, then as now, ℟.

All you holy teachers, in history, in our midst, ℟.

All you prophets in our own age as in ancient days, ℟.

All you artists and musicians of God, ℟.

All you poets, scientists, and doctors, ℟.

All healers, transformers, and bringers of peace, ℟.

All you seekers of the Holy and speakers of the Divine Way, ℟.

All you breakers of the barriers and witnesses to love, ℟.

(Other names and examples of saintly living may be added.)

All You holy ones, named and unnamed, ℟.

All you known and unknown, ℟.

All you who have ushered in some part of the Reign of God, ℟.

O God, let the presence of all Your holy ones endure in us and in our families of Faith. Let their examples of lived love, humility, and wisdom continue to teach and inspire Your people. We pray together. Amen.

A READING

Elif Shafak, *The Forty Rules of Love*

These are words of a sister in the Spirit, Elif Shafak:

"Before passing through the gates of a town I've never visited, I take a minute to salute its saints—the dead and the living, the known and the hidden. Never in my life have I arrived at a new place without getting the blessing of its saints first. It makes no difference to me whether that place belongs to Muslims, Christians, or Jews. I believe that the saints are beyond such trivial nominal distinctions. A saint belongs to all humanity."

Hear what the Spirit is saying to all the Church.

Thanks be to God.

A REFLECTION OR GROUP SHARING

(Some meditation on the feast is given.)

A LITANY OF PRAYERS OF THE COMMUNITY

Let us now lift our voices and offer our prayers for the Body of Christ to God, who transforms our darkness into holy light.

1) Let us pray for the Body of Christ at work in the world, for all those who teach, lead, heal, and minister in the name of Christ.

O God, give Your wisdom and grace to all the Church. Help us in our struggles to be faithful. In work and word, lead us to be living signs of the risen presence of Jesus in our world.

Hear us, we pray.
For we are Your people!

2) Let us pray for all believing peoples, for those who seek the face of God and pursue what is true and good and of lasting value.

O God, be with us all as we seek to find our way. However we name You, in whatever way we praise You, may we be brought together in truth and love. Help us to honor the journeys of faith we each make in our own ways.

Hear us, we pray.
For we are Your people!

3) Let us pray for our country, for our elected officials, and for those who have control over governments, resources, and finances all over the world.

O God, may Your Holy Spirit influence all who make decisions for welfare or for woe in our world. Save us from anger, greed, and the will to dominate others. Grant wisdom to all who lead.

Hear us, we pray.
For we are Your people!

4) Let us pray for the poor, for the body of Christ in need in the world, for all those without homes, without jobs, without the means to live in freedom, for all those burdened by life's cares.

O God, stand with those who stand in need at this hour. Help us to be the presence of Jesus to those around us who need care, sustenance, clothing, safe dwelling, and companionship. Make us generous. Help us to remember Your love for all people. Give us eyes to see the human soul.

Hear us, we pray.
For we are Your people!

5) Let us pray in thanksgiving for both those who have been part of our journey toward holiness in the past and all who are part of our journey today.

O God, we thank You for all the holy men and women who are a part of our lives. For saints and sinners who have shown compassion and wisdom, understanding and courage, and, above all, love in their lives. For the people who matter to each of us who are signs of Christ's body in our day.

Hear us, we pray.
For we are Your people!

6) Let us pray for the sick and the suffering, all members of the body of Christ who are in need of healing.

O God, surround with Your healing power all those who suffer from physical, mental, and spiritual affliction. Give strength and compassion to those who give care to people in our homes and hospitals. We especially ask Your blessing for those whom we name at this time:

(Please name aloud those persons in need of healing.)

Hear us, we pray.
For we are Your people!

7) Let us pray for the dying, all members of the Body of Christ who are making their passage to eternal life.

O God, surround with Your grace those who are dying. Help them on their way. Sustain those who minister to them in hospices and homes. May those who feel forgotten or who are abandoned at the hour of death know Your loving company. Cradle in Your care those who have come to the end of life through acts of violence or neglect. Grant Your presence to

At the Old New Year

all those about to die, especially those whom we lift up to You now:

(Please name aloud those persons who are near to death.)

Hear us, we pray.
For You are our hope!

8) Let us remember those from our lives, from this community, from other communities, who have died, who have shared some measure of the Reign of God among us:

(We name aloud those who have died in the last year, and we light a candle for them as we do so. Or some may choose to light the candle silently. When all are finished, the following is prayed by all.)

CLOSING PRAYER

Most Gracious One, the prayer of the body of Christ is lifted to You throughout the globe. Let all our voices blend in faith. Let our wills be joined in hope. Let our hearts become one in true charity. We thank You for our connection to You and to one another through Your Son, Jesus. Keep us joined to him, now and always, through the Holy Spirit, forever and ever. Amen.

THE AGAPE

A Reading: Isaiah 25:6–9

A reading from the Book of Isaiah.

On this mountain the Lord of hosts will make for all peoples a feast of rich food, a feast of well-aged wines, of rich food filled with marrow, of well-aged wines strained clear. And God will destroy on this mountain the shroud that is cast over all peoples, the veil that is spread over all nations; God will swallow up death forever. Then the Lord God will wipe away the tears from all faces, and the disgrace of God's people God will take away from all the earth, for the Lord has spoken.

It will be said on that day, Lo, this is our God; for whom we have waited, so that God might save us. This is the Lord for whom we have waited; let us be glad and rejoice in the salvation of the Most High.

Hear what the Spirit is saying to all the Church.
Thanks be to God.

THE BLESSING

Leader: My brothers and sisters, God has graced the body of Christ with many gifts. With bread and wine today, let us remember our connection to one another and to all who have hungered for the fullness of the reign of God.

(Leader lifts bread for blessing.)

O Gracious One, Feeder of the Human Soul, we thank You for this bread and for every other gift that sustains us in body and soul, every day. We break this bread,

(Leader breaks the bread.)

mindful of how the saints of God have been broken in every age for the sustenance of the world. Help us to live the blessing and the wisdom of this bread.

(The bread is further broken and shared around the group, and all eat.)

(Leader lifts the fruit of the vine for blessing.)

O Holy One, Sustainer of our spirits, we thank You for the fruit of the vine that has been crushed and poured out for us, and for every other gift that delights us in body and soul, every day. We share this fruit of the vine,

(Leader pours out the fruit of the vine into a single or multiple cups.)

mindful of how the Saints of God have poured out their lives and their love in every age for the nourishing and preserving of the world. Help us to live the blessing and the wisdom of this fruit of the vine.

(The fruit of the vine is shared around the group, and all drink. When all have finished, the following is prayed by all:)

Let us pray:

> **We praise You, O God, for in this company, once again, You have strengthened us with Your Word. You have fed us bread of the earth and given us a cup of hope and freedom. We remember that, through Your Spirit, that limitless power of Love, we are connected with all who have come before us and with all those who come after us.**

> **Keep us connected to You and to Your whole created family, that we may live lives worthy of our calling in You and grow in fullness of heart and spirit through Christ Our Lord.**

> **Amen.**

Leader: Let us close our prayer with a sign of peace.

(All share some sign of the peace of Christ.)

■ ■ ■

November Meditation and Reflection

All Souls' Day

APPLICATION

For personal or communal prayer and reflection on or around November 1 or 2.

SET UP

This can be prayed in any setting, but it can be especially effective in an informal circle, around candlelight or even a fire. The reflection questions can be used for journal writing or for sharing in a group. The stanzas of the prayer can be read by a single reader or read aloud as a group.

CALL TO PRAYER

The prayer begins with some sort of call to mindfulness (quiet, intentional breathing). Music, leaves and branches, an image of the resurrection, a lit candle, and perhaps some incense may prove helpful.

Merciful God,
It is November:
Earth turns slowly toward
her stately dying.
All the green of summer
has blazed past ripe
    fruition and
crumbles now
into inevitable brown.

The world is brittle, ashen,
a cold place, easily broken,
swollen with memory.

Close-knit within each of us in
this dying season
are the strands of lives of
those we have loved,
lustrous histories of
those who have touched us
by their words, their caring,
their long struggle.

As we lifted them once to
cold cradle in the earth,
so now we lift them to You:
their fragility,
their suppleness,
their strength.
We place their souls
    into Your hands;

lift the parts of them
breathing still in us
again
into Your hands,
into Light,
into the great embrace
   of Your Love.

Ever-living One,
for all they have been to us,
for the ways they have
marked our lives,
brought us into knowing
the gift of our days
and the dearest delicacy of
our own brief lights:
We thank You.

For they are not
the dying of the earth;
they are its fullness.
Our loves
are not
the ending of a season—
stone doors
closed against us.
They are the near-silent life
ever-growing within us.
Gifts of perpetual giving,
they are the wisdom
   of the earth
speaking through
   the inevitable snows,
more green than spring,
with promise more lasting
than summer.

We commend them to You,
over and again,
O Limitless Love.
Let light shine upon them.
Let them embody always
the brilliance which,
for a while,
they had been for us, here.

Thus may our not-long dance
of sleeping and waking
be measured hopefully
ever onward,
deep into that Lasting Day
when joined circles of
all Your Sons and Daughters
greet You together,
like stars and swirling suns
set to dancing,
with glad and endless praise.

AMEN.

FOR WRITTEN OR SHARED REFLECTION

Of those who have died:

- *Who remains in me still?*
- *Who continues to matter to me consciously?*
- *Who has shaped me significantly?*

Who has been a particular gift to me?

- *To myself as a human being?*
- *To my profession or to my ministry?*
- *To me as a mentor, guide?*
- *To me as a friend?*

With whom do I most long to be reunited? Why?

■ ■ ■

All Souls' Day Prayer Service

In Remembrance of Those Past

APPLICATION

All Souls' Day gathering (November 2)

SET UP

This prayer works well within a circle in an open room. A circle within the circle, or set of circles (a Mandala), can be established with the paschal candle in the center of the space, four large candles (for the gospels or the directions), a wreath on the floor made up of branches, fall leaves, harvest fruits, additional candles, etc. Photographs of the dead—recent, ancestral, related by blood or by story, global or familial—may be placed in the circle as people gather, or the placement of some or all of these items can be done as part of the call to prayer. All have a copy of the text. Be ready to play recorded music if that option has been chosen. Where resources and talent exist, live music would be great for building the experience and the community.

The prayer can be read antiphonally on two sides, or other designations can be made. The parts in bold are read by all.

CALL TO PRAYER

The prayer can begin with an explanation of the feast, its history, and its potential meanings for us. There is some sort of call to mindfulness (quiet, intentional breathing). This may move into some instrumental music or appropriate song. A leader begins the prayer when all are ready.

INTRODUCTION

Leader: May the peace of the Most Loving and Eternal God be with you.

And also with you.

My friends, we gather in this place today, with our different traditions, convictions, and beliefs, to remember those who have passed, to give thanks for their presence in our lives, and to recall the frailty and brevity of our own walks on the globe.

As we lovingly remember those who have passed from this world, let us be mindful that God, who transcends nations, times, and the boundaries of death, is present in our gathering, eager to nourish and strengthen us so that we may live fully in the world that is full of the mysteries of life, death, and what may be beyond.

In quiet, let us open ourselves to the Presence of the One who would speak to our hearts.

(There is a moment of silence. Then begin the following invocation.)

AN INVOCATION FOR DIA DE LOS MUERTOS

Leader: So, together we pray:

**Come, Great Spirit,
Holy Mother of the Earth!**

Be with us as we stand
in the circle of
Holy Remembrance.
Cradle us
in Your great embrace
and hold us close to You.
Protect us and keep us.
Surround us with
Light and Love.

**Come, dear spirits,
Mothers of our mothers,
sisters, cousins,
daughters, aunts!
Fathers of our fathers,
brothers, uncles, sons!**

Be with us as we stand
in the circle of
Holy Remembrance,
Tied together by
blood and place,
Linked by tenderness
and struggle.
Known and unknown,
Come close to us,
As we remember you
in Light and Love.

**Come, dear spirits,
Soul companions,
Friends of the heart,
of the mind,
of childhood, of now!**

Be with us as we stand
in the circle of
Holy Remembrance,
Brought together by history
and incident,
Linked by laughter
and shared tears.
Familiar and mysterious,
essential spirits,
Come close to us
as we remember you
in Light and Love.

**Come, dear spirits,
Teachers of our teachers,
Mentors, poets,
artists, dreamers:**

Be with us as we stand
in the circle of
Holy Remembrance,
Drawn together by schooling,
writing, speaking,
Bound by ideas and visions,
passions and hopes.
Shapers of our journeys,
come close to us
as we remember you
in Light and Love.

Come, gentle spirits!

Never far from our hearts.

Come, guiding spirits!

Never far from our souls.

Come, loving spirits!

Who dwell in Light.

As we remember you,

**May we ourselves
be made whole.**

As we tell your story,

**May we know better
our own.**

Be a part of us anew,

**For you are ever
a part of us.**

Loving One,
Who holds all
In that place that is
beyond time,
beyond space,
beyond our comprehension,

**bless this time,
our stories,
our fellowship,
our unfolding,
always in Your Love
and Light.**

Amen.

A TIME OF CONTEMPLATION

(During a period of silence or soft music, we consider:)

- Who has passed from my life?
- Whom do I remember?
- Who especially matters to me?

- What gifts did she/he/they give to me?
- What gifts do I still feel present?
- What brings her/him/them to mind for me?
- Why do I honor her/him/them?

(This reflection can be written in a journal; or, if time, space, and resources allow, one can reflect by drawing, painting, making a collage, etc.)

A TIME OF SHARING

(We share with one another [in pairs or triads] the people who came up for us during the reflection, or perhaps the impact of remembering. The leader gives an indication of time allowance. When sufficient time for sharing has passed, the leader introduces the next part.)

A LITANY OF BELOVED NAMES

(After the group remembrance, we reform the circle (candles may be distributed to each participant). We go around the circle; each speaks the names of those we wish to remember. Each participant may light a candle at the naming.

After each person has spoken, we all respond: **You are remembered here.** *When all are done, we pray together.)*

PRAYER

Leader: Let us pray:
O Gracious God,

**As we stand now in
Your presence,
we give thanks for
the gift of memory
and the people who
matter to us.**

**In this circle here,
  we remember
that we stand
  in a much larger,
mysterious, and
  wondrous circle.**

**We stand with
  the company of
all those who have
come before us.**

**We stand with
  our families:
Parents we have loved,
Children we have lost,
Brothers and sisters,
and generations of
named and nameless
  relatives,**

All gone before us.

**We stand with our friends,
with our teachers,
with our loves.**

**We stand with
the anonymous poor,
the martyred and
the murdered,
the forgotten and
the abandoned.**

**We stand with
the powerful and the holy,
with the forgiven
and the unawakened,
with the wise and the
compassionate.
We stand with
saints and angels
and all the women
  and men
through history,
with the human
and the creature,
with the outspoken
and the voiceless,
with the blessed
and the seemingly-damned.**

**In this moment of
Re-membering,
we stand
to name You, again,
Our Maker,
Our God over all
and in between all,
the living, the dead,
and those to come.**

**Keep us bound together
in Your love.
Make us mindful of
our timeless connection
in You.**

Amen.

WE SHARE A SIGN OF PEACE WITH ONE ANOTHER

CLOSING PRAYER AND BLESSING

Leader: Let us pray:

Holy God Beyond All Time and Space, we live mindful that the gift of this mortal body is not forever. We know our own frailty. We know the passing of those we love. We know that at every moment, people young and old, rich and poor, all over the earth, die in violence as well as in blessed peace. We give You thanks that memory and affection keep us connected to those who matter who have passed from our lives.

(Leader may raise hands in blessing.)

On this Holy Day of Remembrance, we ask in this blessing of You:

Make us receptive to the Mystery of the dance of Life and Death, which we all share.

So be it.

Make us vulnerable to the Eternal Love that cherishes all persons, both living and dead.

So be it.

In all our living, help us live with appreciation for our lives, with respect for the living and for the passing of all who are connected to us.

So be it.

May the blessing of the Most Infinite, Most Loving, and Most Wise God be upon us, and within us, and among us as we go forth. We pray together.

Amen.

■ ■ ■

At the Old New Year

Veteran's Day Meditation

O God of All Nations, of all the
    bruised and fractured globe,
on this November day
I am here, safe and settled
    in my home,
in a land that struggles with
    its freedoms, trying to stay
    free enough for everybody.

I am here in my homeland
on a day where those who have
    been to battle are honored,
    remembered,
mourned anew, admired,
    or forgotten in the wake
    of bank holidays
    and special sales.

I am here enjoying the luxury
    of conflict at a distance,
    with the morning news
that reminds me every day
    that conflict and battle,
    bravery and wounds
    and loss,
are the bitter bread of every day
    for so many.

For them, it is no holiday.

All I know of battle
    is thirdhand at best:

    photos from history books
    and film clips, hometown
    parades with bands and
    flags and limping men;

three brothers playing war
with plastic army men on a
crumpled rug, as black and
white war films played on
the big box television;

the untold stories in the eyes
of my uncles who survived
the Great War, only with
secret parts of their souls
shrapneled with fragments
of their battles, the deep, unnamed sadness in their eyes;

the remembered grim glory
of my brother's flights over
Vietnam, dodging anti-
aircraft and dropping I-do-
not-know-what into jungles,

the relief of his return,

the surmise about strange
ailments dogging him
thereafter;

a friend's frantic departure
to Iraq for medical duty
and the dissolving of a
friendship because the
inequities of our lives were
too great;

the still-fresh wound of my
nephew's decision to take
to the uniform and join a
war I could not support, and
the rancorous family battle
that ensued because we each
believed what we had to.

There are so many untold tales,
burdens never let down,
bloodied intimacies
    I can never comprehend.
They are a secreted society
    to which I have no entry,
I can only see the shell
    of what they have endured.
I have never been in harm's way,
never put the cause of country
    before my own safety,
never really had to agonize
    over belief and commands.
I have questioned our country's
    motivations for war,
even as I prayed for those
    who were the enactors
    of its dread, dire,
    and thunderous orders.

My imagination is insufficient
    for war.
A veil of unreality slides
    between me
    and the television
    when the battle scenes
are in plain view
    and the scores of
dead,
wounded,
surviving, and
collaterally damaged
are tallied in the reports
    that are hurried through
    to make space for sports
    and weather.

But I ache, with an insufficient
    ache, for the waves
    of women and men
who return for miraculous
    mechanical fittings
    of their lost limbs,
who have taken to life
    on the streets because
    nothing really fits anymore,
who have been praised for
    their valor by the country
    by which
they are now underserved…
it seems we know how
    to send our young to fight,
but do not really know how
    to bring them home.

O God of Full Understanding
for those plunged into
    the ordered chaos of battle
    and bathed in its valor
and its madness, embrace those
    who have survived enough
    to return to this land.
Help them to sort
    what must be sorted,
to cherish what is worthy,
to forgive our lack of
    comprehension,
to honor their service,
    their sacrifice,
    so often unknown,
to untangle what war may have
    scrambled within them,
to heal what was gashed, broken,
    lost, scarred, burnt, within
    and without,
to survive the nightmares
    and the rerun memories
    and the insanity of
    modern killing, and to find
    somehow a space in
    the place for which they
    have fought, served, suffered.

For those of us who have never
    left our shores for wars
    and skirmishes,
grant, O Loving One, patience,
    wisdom, compassion,
    and respect,
even in the midst of
    anger, sorrow,
    and conflicted thought.
May those who have served
    not battle again for a home
    in a homeland for which
    they have already so much
    served and surrendered.

    Amen.

■ ■ ■

Saint Cecilia's Day

A Prayer for Musicians

BACKGROUND

One of the oft-named virgin martyrs of the Church, Cecilia became the patron saint of music because, it is said, while musicians played at her wedding, Cecilia, in her heart, sang only to God. She is frequently shown in paintings with a small (portative) organ or a stringed instrument. A musical institute was founded in her name in the city of Rome, and musical celebrations are held in her honor throughout the world.

APPLICATION

The prayer can be used by individuals, ensembles, or choirs. It's fitting before any concert, ceremony, or worship. It can also be part of a musicians' retreat or a community's honoring and blessing of its musicians. Parts in bold are prayed by all.

O Great Spirit,
Whose voice sings
   in the mountains,
whose music is in the wind,
in the fire,
in the water,
in the groaning of the earth,
in the sighing of the grass,
in the whisper of the waves,
in the endless breath of air,

   Make me a part
      of Your music.
   Give my breath the gift
      of grace
   and make my voice
   one with the world
   You have made.

O Holy One,
Whose voice is in the land
   and above the land,
whose music is in the sky,
in the rocks,
in the silence,
in the roar of volcanoes,
in the thunder of the storm,
in the trickle of the stream,
in the beat of
   the hummingbird's wing,

> **Make me a part
> of Your music.
> Give my breath the gift
> of grace
> and make my voice
> one with the world
> You have made.**

O God of Life,
Whose voice is in all creatures,
whose music is
   in the human heart,
in the newborn's cry,
in the last breath of the dying,
in the utterance of lovers,
in the prayer of the searching,
in the unfurling of leaves,
in the sound of
   the earth's beasts,

> **Make me a part
> of Your music.
> Give my breath the gift
> of grace
> and make my voice
> one with the world
> You have made.**

Whether sung or strummed
   or plucked, whether through
   wind or hammer
   or drummed,
Whether large or small, glorious,
   humble, or hardly heard,
make my music one with the
   music of all You have made.
Bless its making and its hearing.

> **Make me a part
> of Your music.
> Give all my efforts
> the gift of grace
> and make my sounds
> one with the sounds
> of all that
> You have made.**
>
> **AMEN.**

■ ■ ■

A Table Prayer

For the Feast of Christ the King

APPLICATION

At the end of the Church year, the Church proclaims that all things are under the servant-kingship of Christ, who came to power through the ordination of the Father/Creator and not by violence. This table prayer is an alternative service for a gathering that is not necessarily clergy-lead and, in its heavily participative structure, acknowledges the shared leadership of all.

SET UP

This is prayed by a group gathered around a single (expanded) table, or at a series of tables. Tables can be set as simply or as elaborately as resources allow. Candlelight and tablecloths are conducive to the sense of a ceremonial meal. Different icons/images of Jesus (Good Shepherd, receiving children, feeding the multitudes, upon the cross, resurrected, etc.) may prove useful/instructive in the expression of Jesus as "king," prime shaper of the Reign of God.

At the table, all have a glass and a copy of the text. The fruit of the vine (wine or juice) is distributed to each person's glass at the table. A loaf of bread for breaking is in readiness at a leader's place, or loaves of bread can be present at each table.

Individuals read the numbered portions (this can be designated in advance or done spontaneously). All read the parts in bold type.

CALL TO PRAYER

The meal begins with an indication of the nature of the prayer, a touch of history, and some sort of call to mindfulness (quiet, intentional breathing or meditational music or a song). A designated leader lights a candle and begins the prayer when all are ready.

1) Let us now, in a moment of silence, place ourselves in the presence of God,
whose mercy and strength are with us, guiding us, even in the midst of difficult and confusing times.

(We pause in silence as candles are lit.)

The peace of Jesus, Our Risen Lord,
be with us all.
**The peace of Christ reigns in this room
and in our hearts.**

2) Welcome to this holy place!
Welcome to you, saints and sinners,
wise and foolish, great and humble.
Welcome all to the Reign of God!

3) You who hunger for the face of God,
you who strive for holiness and for wholeness,
you who await the fullness of God's Reign,
you are all welcome here.
**We are God's people.
We have come to the table
to celebrate the One who calls us
and to praise Christ,
the joy of our salvation.**

4) My brothers and sisters, in our prayer tonight,
we complete our liturgical year, celebrating
the fullness of the Reign of God
   in the person of Jesus.

5) Scripture reminds us that the Reign of Christ does not conform to patterns of earthly power and grandeur.

6) The throne that Jesus approaches is the exalted place of the cross. And the model of leadership he gives us comes from one who knows us intimately, even in pain and death.
> **Here in this room, Creator God,**
> **We, who are among the inhabitants**
> **of the Reign of Christ, gather around**
> **the bread that is to be broken**
> **and the wine that is to be poured out.**

7) At this table we poor and strong, we rich and lowly, we wounded and able, lift our hearts in thanks and hope to You who have called us here.
> **For we remember Your Son:**
> **Blessed over ages,**
> **Servant of the bowed down,**
> **Challenger of the proud,**
> **Lover of the poor,**
> **Shepherd, Holy man,**
> **Teacher of the People,**
> **Binder of the wounded world,**
> **And irritant to empires of earth.**

8) Through the power of Your Spirit, all the earth awaits the fullness of the Reign of Christ,
> **Whether we know it or not**
> **the longing in our deepest hearts points**
> **to our emptiness and our yearning for the**
> **presence of the One whose coming we await**
> **each day to ease the suffering of humankind,**

9) to bring an end to our battles and our fruitless wars, to end our poisoning of Your great gift, to show us how to lay down our arms, our angers, our violence and rage.

10) Most Holy One, in Your Son, Jesus, You showed us the way to holiness through the washing of feet, the serving of the lowliest, and the loving of the unwanted.
> **In Jesus, You showed us**
> **the path of perfection,**
> **Through the regard for children, the respect**
> **of women, the embrace of the outcast.**

11) In Your anointed one, Most High, You showed us the path to the place of power and strength by his taking on all that is human, by accepting mortality, by laying down his life for his friends, for us all.
> **By embracing death, he has become for us**
> **the source of everlasting life**
> **and the crown**
> **of Your great work of Creation.**

(The bread is lifted in blessing.)

12) We remember how, in the company of his companions, on that night before he died, he took bread and broke it, and in doing so he broke open the gates of the place where he would reign;
> **and so to remember him,**
> **we bless and break**
> **and share this bread,**
> **that the Reign of Christ**
> **may come among us.**

(The bread is broken and passed for sharing. All eat.)

(The cups of the fruit of the vine are lifted in blessing.)

At the Old New Year

13) And we remember how,
after supper, he took the fruit of the vine
and poured it out, and in doing so,
he poured out the strength of his Reign, which
would flow through his people forever.
> **And so to remember him,**
> **We have filled these cups**
> **with the fruit of the vine.**
> **We bless it with our thanks**
> **and share it with one another,**
> **That the strength of Christ**
> **may be among us.**

(We take a taste of the fruit of the vine.)

---

14) Called to follow Jesus,
we ask you to help us to reconcile and unite.
Together with the whole Body of Christ,
may we help to bring about
the fullness of Your Reign.
> **For Yours is**
> **the Reign of Christ,**
> **the power of Christ,**
> **the love of Christ,**
> **and the glory of Christ,**
> **in the possibilities of**
> **the Holy Spirit,**
> **O God Eternal,**
> **now and for ever.**

AMEN.

■ ■ ■

Our Daily Bread

A Prayer of Gratitude Near Thanksgiving

APPLICATION

On or near Thanksgiving Day. Near Harvest. Any day of thanks-giving.

SET UP

This prayer can be done at table (dinner table) or in a circle where a small table can be placed in the middle of the group in an open room. The table can hold a candle (or candles). It can hold the traditional symbols of harvest or symbols of a harvest particular to the group that is gathered (photographs, written materials, images, etc.). Provide pens/pencils/markers and slips of paper that may be as simple or as decorative as is liked. A basket may be used to collect the expressions of gratitude that will be written down later during the prayer. All have a copy of the text. Be ready to play recorded music if that option has been chosen. Where resources and talent exist, live music would be great for building the experience and the community.

The prayer can be read antiphonally on two sides, or other designations can be made (e.g., leader/all, with the parts in bold being read by all).

CALL TO PRAYER

The prayer can begin with an explanation of the gathering, the larger feast, its history, and potential meanings for us. There is some sort of call to mindfulness (quiet, intentional breathing). This may move into some instrumental music or appropriate song. A leader begins the prayer when all are ready.

POSSIBLE OPENING MUSIC

- *"All Good Gifts"* (We plow the fields and scatter...)
- *"Blue Green Hills Of Earth"* from Paul Winter's **Missa Gaia**
- *"Come, Ye Thankful People, Come"*
- *"For the Beauty of the Earth"*

OPENING PRAYER

Holy One,
from of Old
the earth has been our teacher:

Her seasons,
Her strengths,
Her limitations,
Her abundance,
Her mystery,
and her forbearance.

The gifts she has given
   for our continuance
and for our flourishing
have taught us how to
   be grateful
and have mirrored Your great
giving to us.

You have made us creatures of blessing.

In this time of harvest,
we are gathering
like our ancestors of many lands
and many beliefs

> **Who have been
> on the brink,
> Who have suffered the hard
> labors of the Earth,
> Who have reveled in the
> fruit of those labors,
> Who have grieved
> the price those
> labors have exacted,
> Who have accepted the
> generosity of others.**

We are gathering
to acknowledge

> **That we are not
> the authors of our
> own salvation.
> That there are more hands
> than our own that
> sustain us.
> That in every necessary
> movement of
> our being
> there are forces and graces
> and wonders
> that uphold us.**

We are gathering to say to ourselves and to You:

> **Thank You,**

for there is more gift in our lives
than we can sometimes see.

> **Thank You,**

for there is more that is miraculous than we can sometimes know.

> **Thank You,**

For there is more that is blessing
than we will sometimes say.

> **Thank You.**

So open our lips, our eyes, our
hearts in this gathering, that

> **"Thank You"**

may be more readily sprung
from our truer selves.
Amen.

WE REFLECT AND WE WRITE AND WE SPEAK

We consider those things for which we are grateful.

We remember how we are blessed and gifted.

We recall those people and circumstances that make our lives worthwhile.

(We write these things on the papers provided. We share one-on-one or in the whole group. The "blessing papers" are placed in the center basket for offering. After the sharing of blessings, bread is taken up for the following prayer.)

WE BLESS, BREAK, AND SHARE BREAD

O Thou of Great Giving,
O Hand ever open,
O source of gracious life
and word,

> **Give us this day
> our daily bread.**

O Abundance unending,
O Mother Father of us all,
O Generous and Generative,

> **Give us this day
> our daily bread.**

Fill us with good things,
With Plenty,
With enough.

> **Give us this day
> our daily bread.**

Make us aware.
Expand our hearts with Your
own grace.
Cultivate in us a seed of Your
own generosity.

> **Give us this day
> our daily bread.**

May we share our bread
   with the hungry.
May we open our doors
   to the homeless.
May we unshield our hearts
   toward those in need.

**Give us all this day
   our daily bread.
Give us the Grace
   of Gratitude.
Give us the Grace
   of Knowing
that we each are gifted,
   and how.
Amen.**

(We break and share bread.)

A CLOSING PRAYER

**O Holy and
   Abiding Mystery**

**We give You thanks for
   bread that sustains us,
for companions
   that strengthen us,
and for the manifold gifts
   that You have given us.**

We are sorry that
sometimes we are
so small with our thanks,
so hurried and perfunctory
with gratitude,
as if to say
"Thank You"
were more than we can
manage and
too much a drain on our
   proud self-sufficiency.

Help us to remember
how gratitude expands
   the soul
and lessens our isolation.
How appreciation of even
   the simplest daily thing
links us with the great
Work of Creation
that vibrates
   with awareness.

Let the warmest
   and humblest thanks
be a steady flame
   in our hearts
ready to come to flame
   on our lips.

To say thank You
is itself Your gift to us.
May holy gratitude make
its home in us all our days.

Amen.

OPTION FOR A SIGN OF PEACE AND/OR MUSIC

■ ■ ■

Thanksgiving Day

Our Daily Bread

> **APPLICATION**
>
> This a simple litany to be prayed at the Thanksgiving table. Different parts of the prayer can be read by readers around the table. The prayer can end, and the feast begin, with the simple breaking and sharing of a loaf of bread.

A LITANY AT TABLE BEFORE THE FEAST

Blessed be God
Whose hand opens
to the needy,

**whose grain is grown,
gathered, and crushed
for the hungry.**

Blessed be God
who calls us out
of the pain of isolation,

**who restores us
at table
as one people together.**

Blessed be God
whose Word is alive,

**whose love is
around us
and within us.**

Blessed be God
who gives us
Bread from Heaven,

**who fills us with enough
and grants us
what we need.**

God we praise You,
who alone
has called us out
in love.

**We offer You
all that we are
and give You thanks
for Your abundance.**

Accept, O Gracious One,
our offering of gratitude,

**for all You have done.
We are empty
but now
You shall fill us.**

Amen.

■ ■ ■

Black Friday

A Prayer Before Shopping

O God Beyond
    My Compulsions,
It is the early edge of Friday.
The sun is not yet up.
The house is quiet.
I am alone in the kitchen.
I am charging myself for the
    race of this day's demands.

Hear my prayer
mumbled at the lip
    of this coffee cup
before I tumble unconsidered
into the tasks at hand.

Turkey chills in the refrigerator,
awaiting its second command
    performance as a meal.
There is potato
    (white, fat with butter; sweet,
    crusted with marshmallow).
There is pie
    (apple, pumpkin, pecan,
    unheroic mincemeat).
There is the green bean thing
    (floating in grey sauce,
    denuded of its topping).
There is no dressing
    (there is never enough).
They will all wait for
    my desperate sustenance
    at the end of this day
when, blurry but triumphant,
    I shall emerge, a wraith,
    but accomplished, a victor.

But see now,
the coffee is kicking in, and I am
    beginning to wonder.
Questions emerge and taunt me
    before I go to throw myself
in the doorways
    of big-box stores, and malls,
    and bargain houses.

It is a risk to ask,
    but, be with me
        in this morning inquiry,
and maybe,
help me change my mind.

Family has come that I
    have not seen in ages.
Shall I leave them orphaned
    to the vagaries of another year?

Others have come back home
    to be with their families
    and distant friends.
Do I sacrifice them
    to the sales spectaculars spun
    special for this day?

The sunrise swears to be
    glorious, even rare, this day.
Shall I surrender it to the glare
    of headlights, shop signs,
    the first wave of a migraine?

Somewhere in the gilded
    promises of this day, whose
seduction begins earlier
every year, I hear the ring of
something hollow, and it haunts
me. Can I trust my inner ears?

Is the chant of more-bigger-
    faster-cheaper as melodic
    as I think—or is it only
well-orchestrated cacophony
    that will not deliver all
    that I intend or hope?

Last year, for those I love, was
there all the happiness that was
guaranteed by my stealth and
sleuth and early rising?

Did I assure the health of the
economy the way my pilgrim
ancestors asked me to?

Did my foray into the still-
dark day of this coveted Friday
give me the peace of mind to
welcome Yule, and You, and an
intended joy?

At the Old New Year

Before I bundle on
    my layered shopping gear
and trundle into the crisp air
to key into the car,
to start the passage of miles,
to fill the trunk,
to agonize over the list,
to snag the deals,
to congratulate myself
    over a hurried lunch,
to sprint, sagging
    with aging effort,
to the last deal of the day,
maybe
just stop me?

Grant me a glimpse
    of another way
to show those I love their worth,
their fragile mattering,
their preciousness,
their priceless, guileless gift
    in my life.

Before I slam my body
    into the crush awaiting
    the opening of another
    store door,
to flood with the others
    into the paradise aisles
    of not-really-deals,
grab me
by the scruff of my scarfed neck
or the strained belt of my jeans
or the pinch in my wallet
into a sensible space
where another cup of coffee
    may be sipped
as the too-rarely-seen loved ones
slipper into the kitchen
to laugh,
to remember,
to give further thanks
for another day
of simply loving.

AMEN.

■ ■ ■

Turning Point
A Meditation as Winter Enters

On the day before
    the weather changed,
we worked in the last
    of the sunshine,
raking up brown bundles
    of crunchy leaves,
hauling into the back yard
    a dozen red bins
crammed with maple, oak,
    linden, aspen.

Bending in ways our bodies
    would remember
smartly in the morning,
    we packed them thick,
building up a golden mound
    on the borders of
desiccated hosta, humbled
    iris, stubborn geranium;
    bundling high
the timber-boxed roses
clipped naked of leaves,
    branches, crimson hips.

In fast-fading light, we who have
    no children
were bedding down
    with swift tenderness
this brood of stick-kids,
finally surrendering to sleep
    and anticipated frost.

But, still, the night went gentle.
    In the morning,
pink blooms clung to branches
fierce as baby fists to rattles.

Maybe, we thought, this season
    would endure.

By day's end, the west went wild
    with wind that drove
a grave blue-grey over garden,
    city, plain. At last,
winter would make a mark
    upon land too-long
summered in lazy, forgiving,
    long-lived light.
Darkness was coming home.
    And behind
rain-spattered glass I watched
    the last of leaves
dashing over lawns, furious,
    pursued.

I launched a skyward prayer,
    knowing,
not near so deep as others,
    how winter dark
    and winter cold
mirror too well the world
    and its wide wounds;
"Can we do this? Can we bear
another season of poor
    Persephone's legacy?
Can we last long enough to see
tulip, crocus, hyacinth push
    their promise
past dead leaves layered
    and pressed?"

The sky answered with a blast
    of breath
that rattled the window
    and whispered fiercely:
"You must."

FOR REFLECTION

- What lessons does winter teach me? What am I being taught today?
- What winter lessons am I open to? What do I dread?
- What lessons am I reluctant to receive?
- What of winter leads me to hope? To deeper Mystery?
- What of winter do I receive with gratitude?

∎ ∎ ∎

Part II
THE WINTER PASSAGE

An Advent Meditation

Advice

> From
> heaven
> the LORD
> looks down
> upon the
> children
> of earth...
>
> PSALM 14:2

Look at them:
what they cannot see,
what they cannot perceive,
what they cannot take in,
because they are so afraid…
They make my heart break.

Look at them:
what they will not see,
what they will not remember,
what they refuse to take in…
They make me so angry.

Look at what they are doing
to the planet,
to the sky,
to each other…
I want to smash them to bits.
I want to start all over.

Look at what they are doing
to themselves,
to the earth,
to each other.

I can't get over what a mess
they are making of things!

I want to gather them up
   in my arms.

O People,
Do you know the power
   you have?
How you can make God weep?
Do you know how
   your words sting
and how your bloody attacks
wound me to the core,
to the heart,
to the center from which
   you came?

There is so much dark.

This is not the dark I made,
not the dark of countless stars
and comets' long-tailed run
   across the heavens.
This is the dark of bad choices
and exploded dreams.
This is the light-loss night
of murders and aborted hope,
the snuffing of life,
the strangled cry of
the toppled towers,
and the dried-blood black
of revenge.

Oh People, I am calling to you,
and I ache.
How can I reach you?
How can I touch you?

Send a fire!
Burn it all into cinders.
Scorch it all into ashes.
Send it on the wind into
oblivion:
ashes—from which something
else may rise.

Send a flood!
Break the old promise.
Wash it clean.
Scour and scrub
    and flush it down.
Make a moist place
for something else to grow.

Send a whirlwind!
Blow it all beyond the ends
    of the sky—
a spiral dance of devil winds
to erode what stands so proud.

Send a prophet!
Hard words, wild words,
    harsh pronouncements,
and the threat of the fruit
    of their
own wicked works.

Send a child.
See if they can hold one more
    fragile thing.
See if they will not break
one more vessel.

See if a child can teach.
See if a child can grow
    among them
and not be battered into bits.

See if they will hear
a human voice,
for they have grown deaf
to thunder, wind, fire,
the voice of God unleashed.

Send a child.
They may yet listen
to God's heartbeat
and remember.

■ ■ ■

An Advent Journey
Table Prayer

APPLICATION

Any week of Advent. Alternative Sabbath gathering, parish meeting, family gathering, retreat, ecumenical gathering of several communities, etc. This prayer form lends itself to a potluck.

SET UP

This is prayed by a group gathered around a single (expanded) table, or at a series of tables. Tables can be set as simply or as elaborately as resources allow. Candlelight and tablecloths are conducive to the sense of a ceremonial meal. An Advent wreath is lovely for this, and its lighting may be part of the Call to Prayer at the beginning. If no wreath is available, simple pine boughs on the tables can help underscore the seasonal nature of the ceremony.

At the table, all have a copy of the text and a glass. The fruit of the vine (wine or juice) is distributed to each person's glass. A loaf of bread for breaking is in readiness at a leader's place, or loaves of bread can be present at each table.

Individuals read the numbered portions (this can be designated in advanced or done at table, spontaneously). All read the parts in bold.

CALL TO PRAYER

The meal begins with an indication of the nature of the prayer and some sort of call to mindfulness (quiet, intentional breathing or meditational music or a song). A designated leader lights a candle and begins the prayer when all are ready.

1) O God of Heaven and Earth,
we remember that You have created us all, and
have longed to be with us throughout the ages.

2) We remember Your call through time
    to the creatures of human flesh:
to Abraham, and Moses, to Sarah, and to Mary,
    to our many ancestors, great and humble.

3) You have spoken in darkness and in light,
urging us to know You, daring us to follow You,
inviting us to give what is nameless a name—
in love, in awe, in mystery.

4) You inaugurated the great dance
that over time reveals Your presence among us.

Here on the journey we praise You,
    And we ask You to renew us
    and bring us Home.

5) As we wander throughout the planet,
You have been with us—
whispering Your holy name in the evening sky,
proclaiming Your kindness through the rising sun,
revealing Your strength in mountain thunder
    and mighty rivers.

6) Your Great Spirit fills the earth
and our hearts know You:
in the music of Your created world,
in the silence of the mysterious night,
in the generosity of human beings.
    At the holy places of the earth,
    You speak to us and feed our spirits.

7) At the tables of our journey,
You feed us bread for our bodies
and companionship for our hearts.

8) At the wounded moments of our lives,
You touch us and heal us.
You nourish our souls.

9) Even in our anguish,
You reach out to us.
Even in our pain, You are there.
Even when we think You are gone,
You are with us.

Here on the journey we praise You,
**And we ask You to renew us
and bring us Home.**

10) Now, in our present darkness,
more than ever, O God,
we long for Your presence
and we wait to hear Your voice.

**We are hungry for a bread that truly feeds,
and a Companion who does not stray.**

11) In Your mercy,
extend Your loving hand to all people,
and lead us forward to a table where
we may yet share a common bread.

12) Dream again, O God,
a dream of Your people,
and bring us to Your holy mountain, where the veil of death that divides us may be taken away.

13) Speak again, O Holy One, a word spoken in the silence, in Your voice that hushes our many noises.

**Be born again,
O Tender Emmanuel,
in our midst,
in the very core of our hearts.**

Make Your dwelling place again in human flesh.
Bless our tables. Share our humble bread.

(We lift the bread and say:)

**Bless the bread that we are about to share.
May it serve as a reminder of Your bountiful
care for the earth and its people.**

(We each break the bread, pass it around, and eat.)
(We lift the fruit of the vine.)

**Bless the fruit of the vine
that we are about to share.
May it serve as a reminder of Your power
to renew humankind.**

(We drink of the fruit of the vine.)

14) Lead us on the journey we must make through the night. And feed us with that which truly nourishes. Do not abandon us to ourselves, but rather, lead us to our rebirth in Christ.

**All this we pray in longing and in confidence,
for You are our faithful God, forever
and ever. Amen.**

(Instructions may be given for the potluck, or this concluding prayer below may be recited by a leader. This prayer can also be used at the end of the meal.)

O God, Great Mystery and Sustainer of our lives,
we know You better
when we share with one another
our daily bread, and the drink
that delights and nourishes us.

May our simple feast of bread and wine
keep us aware of all that sustains us
each day in our lives, both food and companionship,
both drink and Presence.

We bless You at this table and all the tables of our lives, and we ask Your blessing as we go forth from this place to continue our Advent Journey. **Amen.**

Let us go in peace.
Thanks be to God.

■ ■ ■

The Winter Passage

Advent Responsorial

A Meditation

APPLICATION

Any week of Advent. Private prayer or meditation. Retreat. Advent Reflection. Reconciliation.

SET UP

If prayed privately, a lit candle may assist the meditation, especially if prayed before dawn or at evening. It is conceivable that a set of images (PowerPoint, video, etc.) could accompany this in a group reflection, with sufficient time to absorb the images. A single reader or multiple readers (sufficiently practiced—language is complex, emotion is strong) could deliver the meditation. It can also be read by two sides of an assembly, as indicated by bold and regular type.

CALL TO PRAYER

The meditation could begin with a call to mindfulness (quiet, intentional breathing or meditational music or a song). An explanation of the reference to the *Rorate Coeli*, from Isaiah 45:8, and the explanation of a Rain Maker may be helpful.

Drop down dew,
  ye gracious heavens.
Let the earth bud forth
  the Savior!

Drop down gracious heavens!
if any be left to leaven us,
holy rain, again on this
unyielding ground of globe,
After so many moist visitations
can you spare a drip, a drop, a
bucket, enough
to let the earth bud forth?

Let the earth…
When the Baptist came 'round
  this year
I heard him stumble
  on upturned chunks
    of hardened ground:
"I hear the carol
  of the charge card," he said,
"Noels of new debt sung up
against old hunger.
Imagine—such famine in
  the land of designer breads!"
He laughed, sour,
a little bitter,
but not surprised,
and shuffled over clay, clotted,
  caked, a remnant
    of a riverbed.
"Prepare!" he croaked,
maybe a little in need himself,
of that heaven-brewed dew.

Drop down!

I know this thirst—
a kind carried in the ears,
   dry day after day.
A brittling crackle of paper,
scratched,
stained with ghosts
   of inked promises:
"Thus I shall change,
There I will go,
This I will do…"
All desiccated intentions,
a breath away from dust,
begging for a second-chance
   revival of
pulp, pigment, power to be
better than I am.

O Voice, known,
   remembered, Beloved,
pour in these shells
trickle, torrent, any single sign
   of wet,
and course
heartward,
soulward,
deepward,
down
into neglected depths
where something waits,
retrograde, now lizard-like,
   but alive,
tongue quick-tasting the dark,
eager for an end of crack
   and parch,
dreaming of ponds
   near paradise.

Drop Down!
Drop Down!

Eyes still upward, still,
scanning winter-blue spans
   of western sky
like a Rain Maker prospecting
wisps of white cloud, greedy
   for shine,
dying for a thunderclap,
any intimation of that
   necessary anointing,
some proof he is no charlatan.

Drop down dew…

Not another day of dust,
that particulate, gritty pain.
Not another breeze brown
   with exiled soil
searching for damp territory.
Not another acrid,
sun-drenched day with
   flat shadows tacked on sand.

Dew!

Ye heavens, be not like us,
arid, indifferent, unyielding,
barren, bulging, bound within,
better-self kept hidden from
the thirsty outer world.

Master a mercy from
another Source
and shower down what we cannot
manage for our selves.
Tender yourself, O heaven, and

Let the earth
bud forth the Savior.

It is that Promised thing—
that begged-for commingling
   of earth and sky,
flesh and fire,
to which, still, we cling
and wait for soul to see.

Heavens
teach us how to sing;
puddle up in our hollow spaces;
let rivers run again
   and sweep us,
wet and washed,
to Home.

FOR JOURNAL, REFLECTION, OR SHARING

- What dryness do you feel within you this Advent?

- What moisture might you need the heavens to drop down?

- Are there any Rain Makers around you? Are they trustworthy?

- Does heaven feel "tender" to you, to your world, at this time?

- Do you have an urgent prayer this Advent?

∎∎∎

An Advent Prayer

On the Feast of Saint Nicholas

APPLICATION

December 5 or 6. Private prayer or meditation. Group celebration of Nicholas Eve or Day. Gathering of children and adults or a family ministry gathering. Tree lighting ceremony.

SET UP

An icon or image(s) of Saint Nicholas. ("Saint Nicholas" might make an appearance.) Winter treats might accompany the mediation—including gold foil-wrapped chocolate coins (per the legend of his assistance with the dowries of three young girls). Prayer can be copied and printed onto cards.

CALL TO PRAYER

The meditation could begin with a call to mindfulness about the business of Yuletide gifting traditions. Someone tells the story (stories) about Saint Nicholas. There could be an exhortation about generosity of spirit, alternatives to thing-giving, etc.

God of Abundant Giving,
Source of my Being,
Companion to my journey,
Lover of Humankind:

In Your boundless love,
warm my heart in this winter season
and teach me to be generous.

In these days of Christmas preparation,
clear a space in me
free of the clutter of worry and anxiety.

Open my mind that I may be receptive
   to Your inspiration.
Open my eyes that I may see the need
   of others.
Open my spirit that I may respond
   to others freely and with joy.
Open my heart and renew in me the joy
   of wonder,
and restore in me the delight of giving
   to others.

Let me be touched by
that same Spirit that touched
Your servant Nicholas,
who gave without recognition
and served without expectation of return.

Thus may I practice that grace which is
Your free gift to me.
And, little by little,
May I know more clearly
the Great Love
that I seek to celebrate in these holy days
and throughout my whole life. **AMEN.**

A Service of Light and Prayer

On the Feast of Saint Lucy

BACKGROUND

Santa Lucia of Syracuse (283–304), also known as Saint Lucy, died during the persecutions of Emperor Diocletian. Although she was born in Italy, she is especially celebrated in the dark and frozen northlands, where rituals in the pervasive, long times of darkness involve households and villages, special foods, and young girls with crowns of lights and attendant "star boys" in traditional pointed hats. Her day falls on what had been the old date (pre-Christian era) for the winter solstice, and thus her connection with light. Legends of her martyrdom include the removal of her eyes, and so she is associated with sight.

APPLICATION

Any form of personal, familial, or communal prayer, on or around December 13. This service would be especially engaging in an outdoor context, where winter is still a time of darkness, cold, and challenge.

SET UP

This can be prayed by a group gathered around a single (expanded) table or in a circle. All have a candle and a copy of the text. A vessel of earth—gravel, sand, snow—large enough to hold and support the candles is in the center of the space. Litany portions can be read by a leader or shared by multiple readers. Traditional Saint Lucy bread/buns and hot chocolate would be a nice way to end. All read the prayers in bold.

CALL TO PRAYER

The history of the feast can be shared. Call to mind our connection to the earth and its seasons, and awareness of pre-Christian roots to many of our celebrations and prayer. Start in as dark a space as possible. Be mindful of darkness: what it holds, its mystery, its fearful qualities. Imagine what it would be like to live in a place where darkness was so pervasive an element that communities would pray for the return of light. Begin with a call to mindfulness, an intentional feeling of the dark around and within, and move into the prayer when all are ready.

(We are circled in the dark.)

OPENING PRAYER

O God of our Ancestors, like those who came before us, we circle close in the darkness of winter. We circle because the winter is long, cold, and challenging, and the circle gives us warmth, safety, and courage. We gather in the dark to name the fears, burdens, and terrors with which we live, things within us and around us that we know acutely in a time of little light. Together we invite in the power of light, the symbol of You, who are master of every turning of the earth, You who first called out Light and Darkness, and invited us to live fully in all the cycles of our life upon this earth.

A LITANY OF LIGHT AND SIGHT

Abiding God, Author of Creation, You have made both Light and Darkness holy. We know You in the shining spaces and in the uncertain places of the night. On this evening when we long for illumination, we ask You, hear our prayer:

(Individuals read one petition below, or share their own, and light a candle at each petition. The next person in the circle then continues.)

The Winter Passage

From fearful faces of the unknown, **deliver us.**

From doubts about Your presence, **deliver us.**

From shadows that lurk in our minds, in our hearts, **deliver us.**

From forces in the world that unsettle the spirit, **deliver us.**

From worries that come with aging or life circumstances, **deliver us.**

From the uncertainties and pains that rise from loneliness, **deliver us.**

From reservations of stepping out into the darkness of the future, **deliver us.**

(Time is given for people to add their own petitions.)

With the light of generosity and compassion, **help us to see.**

With the fire of wisdom and faith, **help us to see.**

With the illumination of understanding and acceptance, **help us to see.**

With the light of companionship, **help us to see.**

With Your Spirit of creativity and courage, **help us to see.**

With assurance of Your embrace of all, **help us to see.**

(Time is given for people to add their own invocations.)

You who call to us in this and every season, may Your radiance be freed within us and upon all the earth, most particularly where the darkness that is not holy has a hold on human minds and hearts. May Your rising sun be born again in us. This we pray together.
Amen.

THE GATHERING OF THE LIGHT

(We place all our lit candles in the vessel in the middle of the space, and together we pray:)

On the Earth, O God,
 Your Holy
  and Beloved Earth,
 where we each, in our time,
  stand, and move, and act;
 where we each, in our time,
  dance, and love, and die;
On the Earth, O God
 of Light and Darkness,
 we can burn, and scorch,
 or illumine, with the light
  we carry within,
 and the power we carry
  in our hands,
 and the flame we bear
  in our brains, our deeds,
  our words.

O God, as we
 stand encircled,
Touched by Light that
 is born of Your Creation,
we pray: By Your great grace
 —transform us.

Let our light together be
 a healing thing.
a sign of hope to those
 in darkness,
and a power of good
 on the Earth.
where we each, in our time,
 dance in Darkness,
 dance in Light,
 blessed by Darkness,
 and blessed by Light.
Amen.

May the One who is with us
 in shadow and in shining
be with us in this hour
 and bless us as earth turns
 toward its season of Light.

Let us go in peace.
Thanks be to God.

CLOSING

(More candles may be lit, or a fire may be started.

A sign of peace can be shared.

Hot chocolate or mulled cider and Lucy cakes or other treats can be shared.)

■ ■ ■

A Prayer

In the Midst of Holiday Madness

You must understand:
I love birthdays and festivals
    and a party and surprises
    and hoopla
as much as anyone,
but I have to confess
that something has gone awry.
This holiday train has jumped
    its track again
and I find I am the bedraggled
    bundle of rags,
trailing behind an indifferent
    caboose,
a tattered fragment of someone
    who promised
that it wouldn't happen
    this year.

All the required
    seasonal twinkle
has been swallowed
    by a creeping dull shadow.
Persistent carols
(cannibalizing the radio
    since before November)
serve only to jangle my nerves.
Nights have soured so far past
"silent" and "holy" that
no well-intentioned
    angel choir could
recover them from
    the altered states.

You see,
I am the unwilling
    poster child for
the unreflected
    and uncollected masses.
The gloomier consumer,
    the manic merry-maker,
the over-cookied, over-indulged,
    compulsive decorator
(a fake forest of theme trees
    has overrun my home).
My belly bulges from
    unconscious moments
    of mirth.
My teeth ache from a shocking
    surfeit of sugar, and
my feet are a podiatrist's disaster;
they do another's bidding
    entirely,
compelled by a dimly perceived
but powerful agenda.
Even the Internet with its
    seduction of ease in acquiring
has sucked my soul
    and Visa card dry.

So, You understand,
it is not for want of effort
that these hallowed days appear
    neither merry nor bright.
I have done my best with
    the comfortless formula for Joy
and surrendered myself to
    all that Yuletide can require.
So, I am wondering,
as I teeter at the precipice
    of catatonia,

will You forgive me
if, for just a little while, I opt to
breathe
a little consciously,
walk
a little aimlessly,
keep silent
a little secretly,
withhold my well-honed
    holiday skills,
and leave some boxes of tinsel
    and tangled lights
untroubled
in their hard-to reach,
    well-labeled, bulging
    storage bins?

If the porch goes unillumined
    with neon splendor,
can You find me
    in the darkness?
If the holiday dishes go unfound
    for yet another year,
will You dine with me and mine
    in any case?
And if, this go-around,
one less room sits unfestooned
in thematically coordinated,
    neo-pagan perfection,
can You manage to bless me,
    alone or with others,
with the grace of the more-
    perfect sacrament
    of this feast:
a door, opened,
    even if with reluctance,
and a dwelling, lit sufficiently,
    to receive whomever
the night and the unyielding
    demands of the world
    may bring?

∎∎∎

Christmas Card I
A Meditation

APPLICATION

Advent. Private prayer or meditation. Alternative Lessons and Carols.

SET UP

Lit candle, quiet space. This is dense poetic language, with the tone of the angrier prophets. It's packed with images. Allow the images to manifest for you. It may feel counter-intuitive, but allow the tone of the poem/meditation to permeate and resonate in you.

CALL TO PRAYER

The meditation could begin with a consideration about Christmas greeting cards—what do I send? Why? To whom? To what purpose?

After a while, it will not do:
    the gilded hay in manicured mangers,
    the unusually continent cow,
    an oddly blonde Madonna,
    serene and lip-glossed, shining
    in a cottagey barn in Bethlehem.

After a while, you just walk away:
    from Magi, cloaked in awe and ermine,
    unconcerned with goats and
    matted sheep, in a bad part
    of a normally fractious town—
    prettied for the occasion.

You dismiss shepherds, scrubbed
    somehow, freshly showered,
    luminous with comprehension;
    and the Baby, Germanic and gold,
    cradled in the cold, perfectly
    content with the intrusion of angels;
    the unbroken moment of
    intimate adoration, all
    frozen under an orderly
    sequined sky. Why

wouldn't such Divine tidiness
go untrusted
    in an age of mess and mire,
    where in the rusting halls of power
    the liar and the liar's court
    go unchecked? New babies are
    marked for murder on foreign soils,
    their deaths sealed with slight smiles,
    gentle nods, inspired agendas.
    What Gospel will record their
    mothers' cry when our news is
    so tamed and silent? No,

if it's Christ-coming
to be shown,
    let it be in a messy world,
    down the block from the
    churning oil machine,
    angels careening in
    a drone-littered sky,
    frantic with
        an unreceptive world.
    Magi, hard to find,
    wordless in their haste
        to chase down
    stars, prophecy, portents, any
    sign of hope. No,
    not serene infancy, but

let the Baby wail.
    Loud.
    So loud.
    Soul loud.
    So that some may wonder
    what is that sound
    that splits the night,
    no longer silent,
    nor dusted with
        a perfect snow. Let

the Baby wail.
    With a stone-cracking cry
    that could render
        human hearts
    into flesh, for a dew-fresh
    beginning. Yes. Let

the Baby come again.
    Swaddling clothes stained
and ripe for changing; no
less a great mystery to behold
but one less easily packaged,
sold in resin-cast replications,
hand-painted, mantle-ready,
and easy to ignore. Let

the Baby come again, into
the mess we make too readily
    in heaven's name
        and on earth
    as if
    we never heard
        the ancient greeting
    in the first place. Let

all mortal flesh break silence
and remember the call we made
from out of honest woe
    and waiting—
Come dwell with us!
Where *Better Homes*
    and Gardens
we are not, but only flesh,
longing for another chance,
to make of our madness
a better nest
for God's Battered Bird.

■ ■ ■

At Winter's Solstice

That Winter Light —A Meditation

APPLICATION

On or near the winter solstice (usually around December 21). Fitting for personal or communal prayer or reflection. Especially fitting at sunset or sunrise.

SET UP

Both the absence and the presence of light are important. The meditation can be read on its own or can provide a framework for a personal or communal activity. Some indications for activity are indicated in the meditation in parentheses.

Solstice indicates the "standing still of the sun"; the winter solstice is the mysterious and nearly unmarkable moment when the winter darkness begins to tip imperceptibly toward the light. Solstice has its roots in early chapters of the human story. Most of us still marvel when structures like Stonehenge, pyramids, or Mayan temples manifest their astronomical purposes in revealing key elements in the movements in the skies. But what we often forget is that the winter solstice was an indicator that survival itself was possible—in a moment of the calendar year when such a thing seemed nigh on impossible.

This solstice is a useful, if finely nuanced, metaphor for the spiritual life. In a time of darkness, when do we begin to turn toward light? When does grief give way to reclaiming life? Resentment yield to forgiveness? Anxiety and fear turn face to hope? When have we sufficiently dwelt in darkness that we may move into that reliable dance of rising sun and another chance at survival? In Advent/winter we may be more ready to receive word about the possibilities of waiting in night even when we are longing for a new dawn, but (in our better moments) we are aware that both states are crucial for growth and depth.

Perhaps start the meditation as darkness closes in. Allow some time to identify what is darkness in the present moment, perhaps writing down events in personal, familial, work, or global life that seem to represent darkness. As the meditation continues, allow similar time to identify what is light, recognizing that perhaps they are moving in the same time, in the same place, in the same people and circumstances.

(The things of darkness are named—written down and placed in a basket or bowl of earth.)

(I rest in darkness and open myself up to the turning of the earth that I cannot see, but know is happening…)

I've been looking 'round
    at what seems like
the longest end of day,
and I'm dismayed:

Isn't this a new kind of dark
    we're in?
These clouds—aren't they
swollen with a new rage,
grey with a new kind of wrath,
pent-up and cold
    with some anger
        that's beyond ancient,
stained and seething with
warfare that won't cease?

This wind that blows
    'round eaves
and in every in-between
chills and stills human hearts
in a wicked, wild new way.
It seems we have forgotten
a language of gentleness
    or even civility,
and this unkind cold has
sharpened our tongues,
has given a bitter bite to every
word we spit, sputter,
and twitter into ears and ether.

We have ushered in
   a mean winter,
with heavier, harder nights
and brown, bare days,
with grey that hangs overlong
on hearts, heads, flowerbeds—
The only glint or glow caught
on infrequent snow comes from
lamps that are failing.

We are losing track of true
Radiance.

*(Consider at this moment the
incidence of light being swallowed
up in life, on the world stage, the
lives of those around me…Where
does this recognition leave me?)*

I long for that winter light:
the pearl-grey dawn
spun out of crystal,
clinging to grassy fields,
breathing us a someday dream
of crocuses. I crave
the luminous, creamy gold,
neither bought nor sold,
unmeasurable
   in human commerce,
useless, brief, ineffable,
pouring between branches
   of aspen
and birch, blinding me into
birth, and,
Christ-Still-Coming!
How I ache to see
the silver song of sun
dazzling at midday on the breast
of a small white hill,
unmarked with footfall,
its perfect arc echoing
the solar fire that forged
and froze it, and,
before I close my eyes,
let there be again
in the west of a December sky,
bright blades of bloodless
   wounds
spreading across a day's
   more-blessed end,
sinking into plum, wine,
into star-scattered beyond-blue.
Even its clear
darkness
is shimmering.

*(Name the things of light that
are happening individually,
communally, globally. Light a
candle—single or multiple—for
these things. Sit in the light; let it
permeate…)*

O, Holy Mother Over Ages,
pour again into the broken,
bruised, and bruted earth,
that star-touched light of
a Holy Winter—
of life emerging
out of madness,
our madness,
born and bred in our old
and practiced dark.

And over our ice-lined tombs
let rise
the Child's voice,
and the Child's hope,
and the Child's true flame,
that we may be made
of bright and shining
   Flesh again.

*(Name what things of the Child
are happening within. Give
thanks.)*

■ ■ ■

The Winter Passage

Christmas Card II

A Meditation (Dedicated to Kathy Kelly: Peace-Bringer, Hope-Bearer, Fortifier of Faith)

APPLICATION

Private prayer or meditation. Alternative ceremony of Lessons and Carols. The reflection below comes from a consideration about Christmas letters that are frequently sent with seasonal greeting cards. Sometimes their happy (or materially triumphal) tone is hard to take in the face of contemporary realities.

SET UP

Lit candle, quiet space. Admittedly, this is irritated, angry language, with the tone of the prophets crying out against the injustice of rulers and the subjugation of those who are easily oppressed. It's packed with images. Allow the images to manifest for you. It may feel counter to the holiday season, but allow the tone of the poem/meditation to permeate and resonate in you.

    Caution! The tone of this piece is not "Silent-Night" pretty and acknowledges that we oftentimes disassociate the paschal part of the incarnational equation in deference to the romanticized aspects of the birth of Jesus.

CALL TO PRAYER

The meditation could begin with a part of, or the whole of, Isaiah 64:1–9. Although contrary to the more frequent reflections of the season, can I allow myself to name the darkness that may be part of me in this season? What is irritated in me during this season of so many glittering images and so many heightened expectations? Does this irritation irradiate hope— or does it sharpen the edge of hope and help me name the shape of my deeper longings?

Isaiah 64:1–2
O that you would tear open the heavens and come down, so that the mountains would quake at your presence—as when fire kindles brushwood and the fire causes water to boil—to make your name known to your adversaries, so that the nations might tremble at your presence!

What I want to do
instead of, you know,
The Family Letter
about my family
whose formation,
pedigree, and
accomplishments
seem less-than-letter-worthy
these days…

What I want to do
instead of the
perfectly confected image
of a moon-lustered snowfall,
that happens rarely
because
winter has grown too warm,
or the photo-shoot woods
and serene fields
have been mowed down
for Walmarts…

What I want to do
instead of that scene
of the immigrant family
huddled in radiance
emanating impossibly
from the golden baby

in coifed curls,
untainted
by birth among
indifferent cows
    and sheep's poo,
and, nearby,
the odd lot of
D-list visitors,
all nestled under
the brute charm
of a hovel, all
pretty, glittered,
and embossed…

What I want to do,
if I were brave
this year,
in this conflicted season of
crucial cash exchange,
in the seemingly endless reign
of an emperor-with-no-clothes…

What I would do,
if it were in me,
instead of images
of the bovine cradle
made dear, made holy,
by a perfect newborn,
is to, instead,

send out crosses.

Post to kith and kin
in this kindest season
of a bitter year,
the rough reminder
that too often,
and still,
we condemn to death

what most we cherish,
and relinquish our assent
to those who can,
by law, leverage,
and sleight of hand
extinguish Light,
thousands of lights,
in the blinking of a dark eye,
made darker in well-crafted
plans
for a legacy,
that each year,
benefits
fewer
and
fewer.

And, mind you,
because,
suddenly,
I found nerve,
I'd send no cross
fit for jewelry
or pious correspondence,
but the proper sight
of the hard tool
government uses to silence
outsider shepherds
who announce
open seating
at a Table
that cannot end,
and a Reign
that bends in service
but not in corruption.

And if, suddenly,
propriety and custom
were to release,
momentarily,
their holiday grasp on me,
I would, myself,
in my own unsteady script
pen season's greetings
that are benediction
or curse:

"May we truly know
our blessings
and their source."

What I want to do,
finally,
is to loosen
my own grip,
to surrender my shoddy
interior real estate
to the hand of that
transforming Prince,
to become a few inches
of that superhighway of
his Table,
crafted from crosses,
spanning the globe,
where I can exchange
bitterness for bread,
blessed by
endless breaking,
passed, hand to hand,
in the clumsy practices
of peacemaking
among strangers
who are learning
to let go.

■ ■ ■

The Winter Passage

Christmas Decoration

A Meditation

APPLICATION

For personal or communal reflection, especially for a tree-decorating event at home or church. This can be used in a gathering of any seasonal storytelling. Perhaps as an alternative to regular material gift giving—"A Night of Storytelling Around the Tree!" Extend an invitation for friends to bring their own seasonal writing or found favorites. Include interludes of hot cider and eggnog—and, of course, fruit cake all around!

Some questions for reflection and additional prayers for home decoration follow this meditation, to be used on their own or in conjunction with the above.

SET UP

Any space that allows people to share readings in a way that they can be heard. It is especially engaging in an informal circle around candlelight, a lit tree (or one awaiting decoration), or a fireplace. Seasonal music is appropriate, of course, but maybe make efforts to pick some of the rich literature of Christmas music that is less well-known (i.e., not played to death on the radio or at malls). Is there a musician available for the evening? Gentle guitar renderings of carols? What can be done to craft a space for remembrance?

CALL TO PRAYER

If the tree is a live one, focusing on the sweetness of its smell may be a good way to begin. What do we associate with pine's fragrance? What memories are stirred? What is our awareness of its history in our homes at this time of year? If the tree is a "perpetual tree" (i.e., out of a box), let other smells (gatherings of fresh pine in a bowl, a scented candle, pine potpourri?) assist your powerful olfactory associations.

When I was very young, before computer games, near the advent of color TV, a little after the Korean War, sometime around the death of the hero in America, I was a deep believer in domestic magic: the kind of magic that is practiced at kitchen tabletops or in family rooms, in seasons of possibility, with those mesmerizing spells that are often accompanied by the powerful words: "If you're good…"

For me, December was the month most charged with this kind of magic. Once snow started to fly (which was pretty early in Michigan), my mind would be spinning with the kinds of questions that make little children ready to see angels, and mothers ready to abandon their homes altogether. I do not know how mothers survive Christmases with eager children. "When will it be Christmas? When can we go downtown? How soon 'til we pull out the nativity set? Will Grandma and Grandpa come over on Christmas? Are you gonna bake anything? Are we gonna get stockings this year? Can we open a present before Christmas Eve? When are we going to get a Christmas tree? When are we going to decorate?

I think I was most eager about

the last items. I think I lived for Christmas trees. There was nothing so extraordinary in our house at any other time of year. Not even Halloween, with its costumes, or Easter, with its sugary excess, could compare with having a live pine tree with its perfume permeating our drafty house and awash in colored lights (of dubious electrical safety), its branches laden with the fragile trophies of our family history, crowned with a silver spray-painted star with blue lightbulb tips that sometimes worked.

My father, I think, strung the lights. My mother, before I took over as a teenager, unearthed from dirty cotton batting the things of glass and paper and plaster that hung, year after year, from the boughs of never-perfect trees. It was she who daily filled the tree's base with water from a Mason jar in the constant battle with our forced-air furnace. And it was she who swept into piles its dangerous fallen needles, growing in number more and more each of the days of Christmas.

So, in late December, in the corner of our living room, with its forest green walls, its dark-tiled fireplace, and the chocolate brown couch (tired from the abuses of six boys), a tree would shine, with light unlike any other illumination at any other time of year. This light could quiet us (at least occasionally) and invite moments of near-reverence, which were unusual in our fractious family. The tree seemed to exude a kind of force that could fend off arguments (a few), invite reverie, and change the entire aspect of our home. This was powerful magic.

Now I am in middle age, in the mini-epoch of post-Pentium processors and e-commerce, sweating out the ozone crisis, waiting for a return of the hero, enduring the reign of the celebrity-du-jour in America. And I am still a believer in domestic magic. Perhaps to my folly, in my home, I place a Christmas tree in every room I can. They stay up until February. I have sold out to theme trees, and worse still, to artificial trees, which never require water and drop less-lethal needles. Their lights still quiet me. The gathered glitter and glass still make me wonder. And, amongst my ornamental excesses, there are again baubles that bespeak the history I've fashioned with those I love.

There have been years when I felt too sick or too busy for Christmas trees. Advents have arrived when I am too soul weary for decoration. Yuletides have come when I thought myself incapable of untangling another string of lights; but something in me will not allow myself a house untouched by these customs of mixed pagan and Christian ancestry that are dear to me. So despite flu, ennui, neglected bills, or exhaustion, a tree, or two, or three, sprouts up to dispel my apathy or mock my calendar of things to do. I cannot keep my halls undecked, even if I end up cramming for "Decorations 101" on Christmas Eve.

I have asked myself, "Why do I need to decorate?"

Friends tell me that I am just obsessive, and Christmas trees are, at least, a prettier vice than gambling or video games. But I think the roots of this drive in me are deeper. The hunger is for something more than just "pretty." The need is more urgent than keeping up with last year, or Martha Stewart, or the neighbors next door. You see, I think the whole decoration thing is about transformation.

This seasonal proliferation of lights, the abounding baubles,

The Winter Passage

the glass, the glitz: all are pale mirrors to the change we want in the world. However tasteful or gaudy, they come in the year's darkest time as a reminder of something unusual, beautiful, and luminous—an intimation of perfection.

It's helpful to remember that the ancestor to our decorated Christmas tree is the Paradise Tree. Our embellished pines, real and fake, are suggestions of what has been lost, echoes of what may yet be saved in us. To me, it's an act of hope to place such a tree in the heart of our homes, and an act of prayer to sit wordless in its light, in a darkened room, open to our memories, our aspirations, and wonder.

When in December I turn out my home in candlelight and greens, when I hang a circlet of spruce on my front door, or jam sprigs of boxwood, holly, or cedar over picture frames, I am making my little pilgrimage to what may yet be, my journey to a Christ-come self.

To be sure, when surveying the many boxes of accumulated holiday décor, I get a little impatient with my manic changes in surface and my frequent neglect of substance. I ask myself (still), when will I really be transformed? When, instead of trees with electrical lights, might I be a source of illumination? When, instead of ornament boxes unearthed from the basement room, will I bring forth interior treasure to share more freely? When, instead of my terra-cotta Peruvian Nativity Set on the mantle, will others find in me Love's own story played out with straightforward, in-the-flesh simplicity?

Over the last few years, I've watched more neighborhoods glow with more holiday lights. I see Christmas trees in house windows, seemingly earlier each November. I think more vehicles on the road sport those happy, beribboned wreaths in their front grillwork. I wonder if it is all a matter of typical American overkill—or are these folks hungry for transformation too? Are we each striving, in some sort of Yule-driven abandon, to shed light, to give hope, to share beauty, to proclaim possibilities?

I confess, I have bouts of cynicism that mock such thinking. The evening news casts shadows of doubt over cities illuminated with colored lights. My impatience with myself gets transferred to my neighbor. I get discouraged that the "when" of real change will never come to be. I fear that we have grown indifferent to the spirit of the season, and that our hunger for commodities has extinguished our hunger for one another's companionship.

But then I see another tree go up in someone's front window, and my hope about humanity gets a tiny jump-start.

My hope is that each of us is exercising our gifts at changing the world. My hope is that all the winter festivals with their inevitable lights and baubles help us realize the power that is waiting to be born in us. I hope that the bright trappings work their domestic magic on us and reveal, to ourselves and to the world, some deeper beauty we are still capable of bringing to birth.

FOR JOURNAL, REFLECTION, OR SHARING

- What sights, smells, tastes, or sounds stir up memories that I cherish this time of year?

- What kind of feelings do these memories elicit in me?

- Are the memories a burden or a blessing?

- As I remember things over the years, can I see any changes?

■ ■ ■

A Prayer

Before an Undecked Tree

O Wonderful, Ever-Living One,
source of ever-green and
sustainer of fragrant life
in the midst of cold,
and brittle,
and dry,
and dark,

This green impossibility
in this home,
(hall, church)
this cozy space,
this aching space,
this ample space,
this tiny,
waiting,
crowded
space,
needs nothing really
but the attention brought
   to sustain it
in its brief sojourn in this place.

It is its own sign of the Force
   that endures when season
   and circumstance tell it
      otherwise.

Its roots are more ancient than
   we know (even if it has
   sprung from a battered box
   again for us this year).

This tree is a story we tell
   to ourselves
over and again—that,
   despite all that
weighty winter brings,
we may yet survive.

And, for a while, we may even
   be glorious, because life is
   shining near us
and in us.

And so
we rejoice over green branches
(even if their trunk and stems
   are metal),
and we thread the green
   with strings of light
borrowed from stars,
from flame,
from heart,
from history.

We heap our gathered
   treasury of
memory, dream,
folly, and tenderness
to make of this shrubbery
a Beacon of Paradise
in our midst.

As our hands,
whether withered, fleshy,
tiny, or twisted,
practice this old
   and beloved craft,
help us to remember
with joy and gratitude
childhoods that may
   have passed
and people who have shaped
   such beauty in us,
      in our lives.

Grant us the grace
of an animated eye
to take pleasure in what we do
   this night,
as we,
with fragile glass
and shining tinsel,
do
what You can do
with finer stuff
in the human heart.

Amen.

■ ■ ■

A Las Posadas Prayer

A Mobile Meditation

BACKGROUND

With its roots in Spain, Las Posadas is a nine-day domestic celebration (symbolic of the nine months of Mary's pregnancy) observed in villages and towns. It is celebrated chiefly in Mexico, Guatemala, and the southwestern United States. The event begins on December 16 and ends December 24 and generally takes place in the evening (from 8-10 PM). *Posada* is Spanish for "lodging."

Las Posadas generally involves a communal procession, with music, around a community. The procession reenacts Joseph and Mary's search for lodging at the time of Jesus' birth. They knock on many doors, but they are refused entry. After entreaties and rejections at various doorways, the procession finally is welcomed into a house where the nativity is remembered and travelers are given food and drink.

APPLICATION

Las Posadas provides a foundation for many events: a prayer or reflection on immigration; a context for a Lessons and Carols event with music and narration (particularly rich in bilingual communities), an additional lens for understanding the Christmas Story in a grade school, a context for caroling in a neighborhood, an adaptation of "Stations of Christmas" with Scripture and song, etc. Although truer to its roots if a group is moving through outdoor space, the format provided here will also work for a communal ceremonial passage through a house or church, ending with a celebration at a festive table. Portions (*Mary's Posadas Tale*) are also workable for individual reflection. There are lots of possibilities for adaptation!

SET UP

Pathways to or around the space are lined with luminaria (votive candles in paper bags weighted with sand). At the last stop of the procession, a table is set with festive sweet bread, Mexican-style hot chocolate, or whatever "feast" is available for the community. Copies of the text are given to all or to assigned readers. Candles are available for all participants for the final stop of the procession. Appropriate preparations are made for music.

CALL TO PRAYER

Someone explains the tradition of Las Posadas and the purpose of the evening's prayer. Although contemplating the specific search of Joseph and Mary, we are invited to consider the many people around the world who seek entrance into a receptive community, into homes, into spaces shaped by human compassion. Also, in what ways might we ourselves feel on the outside and longing, needing, to be brought in? We are invited to begin the journey of the night with those particular intentions in quiet or shared prayer.

POSITION 1

Call to Prayer

(As indicated above.)

(Music and movement to the second station.)

POSITION 2

Exhortation

Reader: Tonight, we gather in a special Advent journey to retell a very old story, a very crucial part of the whole Christmas story. As we begin, we remember that the Bethlehem journey of Mary and Joseph is also a reminder that the journey of the poor and dispossessed is perpetual, and it is a journey where Christ goes seeking over and over, in human flesh, a place to be welcomed, a place to be born, a place to have home.

Reader: Archbishop Romero once said:
"No one can celebrate a genuine Christmas without being truly poor. The self-sufficient, the proud, those who, because they have everything, look down on others, those who have no need even of God—for them there will be no Christmas.

"Only the poor, the hungry, those who need someone to come on their behalf, will have that someone. That someone is God, Emmanuel, God-with-us. Without poverty of spirit there can be no abundance of God."

Reader: And so in this season of Advent, near the end of another year, let us make room, let us empty some space and allow ourselves this poverty.

Reader: Let us clear a room and allow it to be wanting and waiting for someone to come calling with the plea to enter in and be born.

Reader: Let us make a space within, willing to cradle hope, strong enough to embrace joy, big enough to encourage the first steps of new life.

(Music and movement to the third station.)

POSITION 3

Las Posadas Tale

Reader:
Down the small road,
down through the dust
into the city,
into the night,
they travel together
where the stars are hidden
and faces seem hollow,
all shadowed with fear.

"Try here," she says gently.
"Surely there's room.
Not much,
just a small space,
maybe lighted and warm.
Maybe a bed's near.
Oh, Joseph, I'm weary.
This baby is ready. Knock here,
at this door."

(There is knocking on a door, a post of a space, or a board.)

Like dozens before this one,
the entrance is cold. He knocks,
stands patient and listening,
and knocks twice again.
From the soul of the house
a voice urges,
"Go away, there's no room here,
full up and busy.
You keep going,
the lady, the baby, and all."

He turns, shrugs his shoulders,
takes the girl by the arm,
takes tired steps further
into the
heart of an unyielding town.

(Music and movement to the fourth station.)

POSITION 4

Las Posadas Tale (CONTINUED)

(There is knocking on a door, a post of a space, or a board.)

The Winter Passage

Reader:
"There was room there,"
    she says,
"for certain, enough. Fine space,
and warmth there,
    if perhaps a bit close.
But let's try another.
    Try at this gate.
Joseph, I'm weary.
    My baby won't wait."

(Music and movement to the fifth station.)

POSITION 5

Las Posadas Tale (CONTINUED)

(There is knocking on a door, a post of a space, or a board.)

Reader:
Over and over, at dozens
    more portals,
  come hard-edge refusals
    and the still moving-on.
He sighs at the night sky,
all spangled with stars.
"There's room there aplenty!"
and he wonders how far
that journey to those gracious
    heavens might be,
and if paradise were as closed
as the hearts of earth
    now seemed.

(Music and movement to the sixth station.)

POSITION 6

Las Posadas Tale (CONTINUED)

Reader:
"Joseph," she whispers,
    at the edge of the city,
"there's light at that doorway
where someone stands
    watching.
There are few that may
    travel here.
The road appears rough.
There could be room,
    some space simple
and plain. That's enough.
I'm weary, good Joseph.
    This journey's gone long.
My baby is needing a place
    to be born."

(Music and movement to the seventh station.)

POSITION 7

Las Posadas Tale (CONTINUED)

Reader:
Up the small pathway,
    dimly illumined,
  slowly goes Joseph,
    patient night pilgrim,
pressed down dear
    with the hour
and the travel,
    burdened with need
and sore with denial.

(There is knocking on a door, a post of a space, or a board.)

"My wife there," he says,
    pointing into the night,
"is weary and at her
    appointed time.
All the world
    has shut its doors
against thieves and loves alike.
Tonight, would you have us
just a little while?"

And Mary, round with life,
  wanders near the humble
    light herself
to look up with young
    and urgent eyes:
"Is yours the place
    for my waiting's end?
Does my child find home
    with you?"
and then,
all of history holds its breath,
for suspended in the dark
    and cold,
the weight of gift
    and need, is held
above hands so much our own,
clenched closed or ready
    to hold.

(There is a moment of quiet reflection music and then movement to the eighth station.)

POSITION 8

Prayer

Reader: My friends,
    this story of Mary and Joseph
    is the story of
    thousands and thousands

all around the globe,
   traveling in need and aching
to be welcomed in.

   Together, let us pray
      for the grace to be open:

All: O Mary, Mother of Promise,
   as you made room within
your very self for a glorious
   new life,
   help us to learn how to make
      room for the Christ-coming
   that happens every day,
      quietly and certainly
         around us.

Help us to open up a shelter
   within and around us
for those who stand outside
   our doors,
begging entrance, acceptance,
   a bit of quiet,
or some small nourishment.

Guard us from the greed
   and hardness
howling at our worldwide doors
at which you and Joseph stand
   perennially knocking,
      waiting for entrance.

Make us a people ready and
willing for "God-with-us" to be
born in our life and times anew.

Amen.

*(Music and movement
to the ninth station.)*

POSITION 9

**The Last Station:
The Festive Table**

*(There is knocking on a door,
a post of a space, or a board.)*

*(A door opens, or there is some
other gesture of opening. Light is
brought out to all participants,
who light their candles.)*

Reader:
   My friends, Look!
   Here there is an open door!
   Here there is food to share
   and celebration and care.

   Here Mary and Joseph
      may rest for a while.
   Here Christ may be
      welcomed and birthed
         anew,
   for here is the door
      of our hearts.

   Together, let us pray
      for the grace to welcome
         him always:

All: O Emmanuel,
   Child of the ancient Promise,
   Even though we know how
      tightly we can be closed,
   Even though we know
      the excuses we make
         to keep our defenses up,
   Even though the stranger
      among us makes us
         hesitant to be open,
we will try again to make
   space for You
as you enter our lives
   each day.

Let Christmas this year
   be a celebration of
open doors within us,
open hearts within us,
and more open minds.

Help us to provide
   the nourishment,
the warmth, the shelter,
the clothing,
   and the compassion
that the aching world awaits
   from the children of God.

For we know we are, again
   and always,
the Bethlehem,
   the "house of bread,"
where a holy welcome
   is sought for those
      most in need.

We pray together.

Amen.

*(There is an invitation to the feast
and more music. The celebration
ends with song.)*

■ ■ ■

The Winter Passage

Mary's Posadas Tale

Down the hard road,
down through the dust
into the city,
into the night,
they travel together
where the stars are hidden
and faces seem hollow,
all shadowed with fear.

"Try here," she says gently.
"Surely there's room. Not much,
just a small space,
maybe lighted, and warm.
Maybe a bed's near.
Oh, Joseph, I'm weary.
This baby is ready. Knock here,
at this door."

Like dozens before this one,
the entrance is cold.
He knocks,
stands patient and listening,
and knocks twice again.
From the soul of the house
a voice urges,
"Go away, there's no room here,
full up and busy.
   You keep going,
the lady,
the baby, and all."

He turns, shrugs his shoulders,
takes the girl by the arm,
takes tired steps further into the
heart of an unyielding town.

"There was room there," she says,
"for certain, enough. Fine space,
and warmth there,
   if perhaps a bit close.
But let's try another.
   Try at this gate.
   Joseph I'm weary.
   My baby won't wait."

Over and over,
at dozens more portals,
come hard-edge refusals
and the still moving-on.
He sighs at the night sky,
all spangled with stars.
"There's room there aplenty!"
and he wonders how far
that journey to those gracious
heavens might be,
and if paradise were as closed
as the hearts of earth
   now seemed.

"Joseph," she whispers,
   at the edge of the city,
"there's light at that doorway
where someone stands
   watching.
There are few that may travel
here.
The road appears rough.
There could be room,
   some space simple
and plain. That's enough.
I'm weary, good Joseph.
   This journey's gone long.
My baby is needing
   a place to be born."

Up the small pathway,
   dimly illumined,
  slowly goes Joseph,
   patient night pilgrim,
pressed down dear with the
   hour
and the travel,
   burdened with need
and sore with denial.
"My wife there," he says,
pointing into the night,
"is weary and at her
   appointed time.
All the world has shut its doors
against thieves and loves alike.
Tonight, would you have us
   just a little while?"

And Mary, round with life,
wanders near the humble light
   herself
to look up
   with young and urgent eyes.
"Is yours the place
   for my waiting's end?
Does my child find home with
you?"

And then,
all of history holds its breath,
for suspended in
   the dark and cold,
the weight of gift and need,
   is held above hands
so much our own,
clenched closed
   or ready to hold.

■ ■ ■

As Christmas Passes

A Meditation on Mary: The Light of her Face

> But Mary kept all these things and pondered them in her heart.
>
> LUKE 2:19

Good doctor Luke
scribbled gospel lines
about shepherds
    babbling brightly
their unstoppable tale
of angels clouding up the night
with impossible news
    (sung in early Technicolor
    and celestial Dolby sound),
that—in a world where
governors
and soldiers,
temple priests
and tax collectors,
and, generally,
everybody else
was getting the goods—
something wondrous
at last was happening for them:

A child, wrapped
in not-so-wondrous rags
was born for them,
and this child would save.

Hurry
to inconsequential Bethlehem,
the chorus chimed:
God is doing you something grand!

And there,
do you suppose,
at the manger,
his mother,
barely more than child herself,
received these
wooly visitors
(like so many in those days)
how?
A little stunned
but courteous?
Or unflapped
by another set of
eyes at the doorway?
As if this were the course of things
(after Gabriel and all)?

And the words,
do you suppose,
and the wordless questions,
and the looks that,
after a while,
    needed no words at all—
What of them?

Could it be,
they all became fuel
for the glow of her face
that shone
like Nazarene gold
at the end of day
as she sang into his ears
her quiet low song,
part lullaby,
part prayer,
part prophecy,
part warning,
as she wondered,
as any mother would,
of the path
her child would take,
of those things
that waited for him
in the shadows,
and of the Light
that would guide him
if her own light
were to fade?

■ ■ ■

The Winter Passage

A Table Prayer

For a Christmastide Gathering

APPLICATION

Post-Christmas gathering for home or church or community. Parish meeting, family gathering, retreat, ecumenical gathering of several communities, etc. This prayer form lends itself to a potluck.

SET UP

This is prayed by a group gathered around a single (expanded) table, or at a series of tables. Tables can be set as simply or as elaborately as resources allow. Candlelight and tablecloths are conducive to the sense of a ceremonial meal. Plenty of candles amidst pine boughs on the tables with simple decoration (such as paper stars) can help underscore the seasonal nature of the ceremony. At the table, all have a copy of the text and a glass. The fruit of the vine (wine or juice) is distributed to each person's glass before the prayer. A loaf of bread (a sweet, holiday loaf like challah or panettone) for breaking is in readiness at the leader's place, or loaves of bread can be present at each table.

Individuals read the numbered portions (which can be designated in advanced or done spontaneously). All read the parts in bold.

CALL TO PRAYER

The meal begins with an indication of the nature of the prayer and some sort of call to mindfulness (quiet, intentional breathing or meditational music or a song). A designated leader lights a candle and begins the prayer when all are ready.

Leader: Do you know that God dwells within you?
Yes. Indeed. And also within you.

Can you lift up your hearts?
We are ready.
We can lift our hearts to the One
who has made us.

Have you a voice to give thanks to God?
Listen. Hear us!
We are here to speak
and sing our praise.

(Sing a carol refrain—e.g., "Angels We Have Heard On High.")

1) Creator of the Universe,
we give You glory and praise,
thanks and blessing, through Jesus Christ,
whose birth on our Earth
we remember at this table.

2) You have fashioned the planet
   and all growing things
on the land and in the dark waters of the sea.
You have spangled the heavens with stars and whirling mysteries.

3) Out of love
You molded us women and men from the very stuff of the earth
to share in the richness of all things made.
Bold with joy, or tentative and shy,
We praise You, God our Maker,
and bless Your Holy Name.

(Sing a carol refrain.)

4) In space and time, Your Word became flesh in Jesus Christ, whose birth was not unlike our own,

whose bread and sorrow we share, whose word
and promise enliven us.
> **His life brings wisdom and
> good news to our lives.
> His death uncovers
> the truth of our own death.
> His rising liberates us
> more than we can name.**

5) He is for us the Wonderful-Counselor
and the longed-for Prince of Peace.
> **He is the Child of Earth
> and the Son of the Most High.**

6) He is the Bridge of Heaven and the Teacher of
the Human Soul.
> **Humbled by Mystery and curious
>   by our nature,
> We praise You, God of Jesus,
> and bless Your Holy Name.**

(Sing a carol refrain.)

7) Over the expanse of human history
You have set signs in the heavens
and shining wonders in human hearts
that we might find a way to You.
> **In Jesus, our longing finds its home
> and our hearts find healing.**

8) In this feast of Your Midnight Son,
we join our voices with shepherds
who called out in awe.
> **We join the chorus of women and men
>   throughout time
> and in every land who have marked
>   this festival
> with song and prayer,
> with feasts and celebrations.**

9) We join with all the radiant angels and the
mysterious heavenly powers to praise You for Your
great gift to us flesh-wrapped on Earth.

10) We strain to give voice to our amazement for
the always-birth of the long-awaited One:

(Sing a carol refrain.)

11) God Most High: Jesus was born of Earth,
fragile, wondrous, full of possibility,
human like each of us gathered here.
> **We believe he came to teach us true freedom,
> to lay down his life,
> to submit to powers in the earth,
> to reveal the Powers of Heaven.**

12) In Your Son, bound in birthing cloths,
surrounded by his family,
by shepherds and beasts of the open fields,
we can recognize the offspring of
earth's other women and men,
and we are in awe.
> **In this Child, cradled with concern,
>   and mystery and awe,
> by a Mother who, like all mothers,
> knew caution, curiosity, hope, and hesitation,
> we can know our own fragility
>   and pure possibility.**

13) And so, Most Holy One,
we are here with these gifts of
gathered grain and the fruit of the vine
that also are sprung from the earth
in simplicity and strength, and we know
    that we are grateful.

(We lift the loaf of bread in blessing.)

14) We are grateful for our hunger, Most High,
for the basic needs that bind us to all of humankind.

**So we bless You and give You thanks
for all bread that sustains,
delights, and heals us, but especially
for this festal bread
with which we celebrate the birth
of the child of Bethlehem,
the House of Bread.**

15) As we break and share this life,
make us mindful of all we share that gives us life
and keeps us strong.

(We break the loaf, pass it to one another, and eat of it.)

(We lift our glasses filled with the fruit of the vine for blessing.)

We are thankful for our thirst, O Loving One,
for the most basic need to partake in that which
binds us to the Earth.

**So we bless You and give You thanks
for every drink that
hydrates, restores, and gives us joy,
but especially for this fruit of the vine
with which we honor
the birth of the One who would pour out
compassion, wisdom,
and healing like a river.**

(We each take a sip of the fruit of the vine.)

16) As we break the bread and taste the fruit
of the vine,
we ask that You make us mindful of all we share
that gives us joy and keeps us alive.

**In seasons of abundance and want,
In times of hunger and fullness,
When we are thirsty and when we
are bathed in moisture,
Give us hearts and souls that are open
to all of life,
Just as Jesus remained open to all
that makes us human.**

17) In sharing fragrant bread and joyful cup,
make us mindful of those
with breadless days and empty cups.

**May we who share this feast today be ready
to bring food and drink
to those who call upon Your Name
to be remembered in their need.**

Leader: All this we pray
In the name of Heaven's Own Gift,
through the power of the Spirit of Life,
to the God of Everlasting Life.

Amen.

*(Possibly sing **Lilies of the Field** Amen.)*

(Instructions may be given for a potluck or other meal, or the concluding prayer below may be recited by a leader. This prayer can also be used at the end of the potluck meal.)

O God, Great Mystery and Sustainer of our lives,
we know You better
when we share with one another
our daily bread and the drink
that delights and nourishes us.

May our simple feast of bread and wine
keep us aware of all that sustains us
each day in our lives,
both food and companionship,
both drink and Presence.

We bless You at this table and all the tables of our lives, and we ask Your blessing as we go forth from this place to continue our Advent Journey. **Amen.**

Let us go in peace.

Thanks be to God.

∎ ∎ ∎

A Grace

After a Christmastide Meal

APPLICATION

Christmastide gathering for home or church or community. Parish meeting, family gathering, retreat, ecumenical gathering of several communities, etc. This prayer form lends itself to a festive or potluck meal.

SET UP

This is prayed by a group gathered around a single (expanded) table or at a series of tables. Tables can be set as simply or as elaborately as resources allow. At the table, all have a copy of the text. The prayer can be split up among any number of readers or antiphonally on two sides of the table.

CALL TO PRAYER

The prayer begins at the conclusion of the festive meal with an indication of the nature of the prayer and some sort of call to mindfulness of gratitude for the feast, the gathering, the delight, etc.

    Participants can be invited to remember some specific thing for which they are delighted or grateful within this gathering or within the Christmas festivities themselves.

    A designated leader begins the prayer when all are ready.

(*We've celebrated together. Now let us pray:*)

Loving God,
ever and always
You seek us out
and beg new entrance
into our messy human existence.

You know how we are made.
You continue to believe in us,
even as we strive to believe
    in You.

May this meal
    that we have shared
remind us of how simply
You enter our lives.

May the bread
    we have broken together
remind us
that You choose to be broken
with and for us
every day.

May the fruit of the vine
that we've poured out
remind us
that You are
    pouring Yourself out
in us and for us
every day.

The Winter Passage

Transform us all,
so that we who have feasted
in joy and happiness,
may live more
with the heart of Christ,
whose coming transforms
   our world.

Open our eyes to
God-with-Us,
especially when that Christ
is wrapped
in human flesh
that appears strange to us,
altered by pain or need.

Grant that we are open
and able to receive
The Christ
at all our tables
all through the year.

Give us grace
to care for one another
and the world around us
with the compassion of
Bethlehem's Child,
who is Lord,
Lover,
and Brother
forever and ever.

Amen.

■ ■ ■

Feast of the Holy Innocents

A Lamentation for Children

BACKGROUND

The account of the massacre of the children of Bethlehem is found only in the Gospel of Matthew, although it has a strong appearance in sacred art and is generally attached to the fuller accounts of the nativity of Jesus. One of its most poignant iterations can be found in the traditional "Coventry Carol," which can be attached to this prayer at some point (one suggested place is indicated).

APPLICATION

Unfortunately, there is an increasing number of reports of children who are the victims of the powers of governments, corporate behavior, war, disease, and domestic abuse. Though it may challenge the expectation of "happy cheer" during the Christmas holiday, this feast day can be a good opportunity to pray for children across the globe who are the victims of powers far greater than themselves. The prayer can be expanded in a variety of ways, including use of news reports, community experience, and so forth in conjunction with the reading. All pray the parts in bold.

SET UP

This can be prayed in a variety of spaces, in a circle, or with an altar table (perhaps with a red drape) with images of children. There are candles lit before the service that are extinguished during the litany below (one candle per petition). A recording of the "Coventry Carol" or, better, a musician to sing it, is in the ready.

CALL TO PRAYER

We bring to mind the presence of God, the great needs of the world, the incidence of violence toward children, and the mercy of God. When all are ready, the prayer begins.

INTRODUCTION

(A greeting, an explanation of the feast of the day, and the focus of the prayer.)

OPENING PRAYER

O God, You are Father and Mother to all the world. Your love knows no limits, and the loss of the innocent is a special grief for all of heaven. The children of this planet have always been at risk. They become the victims of government will, corporate indifference, incessant war, rampant disease, and domestic abuse. Hear us this day as we lift our voices on their behalf; and in our prayer, move us to action. This we pray. **Amen.**

A READING

THE MASSACRE OF THE INFANTS (MATTHEW 2:16–18)

When Herod saw that he had been tricked by the wise men, he was infuriated, and he sent and killed all the children in and around Bethlehem who were two years old or under, according to the time that he had learned from the wise men. Then was fulfilled what had been spoken through the prophet Jeremiah: "A voice

The Winter Passage

was heard in Ramah, wailing and loud lamentation, Rachel weeping for her children; she refused to be consoled, because they are no more."

So ends the lesson, but the lesson never ends.

Lord have mercy.

MUSICAL REFLECTION

"Coventry Carol"

(Option for a reflection.)

LITANY OF LOST LIGHTS

(After each petition, a candle is extinguished.)

Let us recall the children in our world who, each day, are lost to violence, warfare, disease, and indifference. We extinguish a light at the naming of each circumstance, aware of the light of potential that is extinguished with each death.

Let us pray:

1) For the children killed in the bombings of the innocent,

Lord Have Mercy.
(A candle is extinguished.)

2) For the children taken in the violence of sexual trafficking,

Lord Have Mercy.
(A candle is extinguished.)

3) For the babies dying because of malnutrition and lack of clean water,

Lord Have Mercy.
(A candle is extinguished.)

4) For the children whose childhood is destroyed because of violence in our homes, in our schools, and on our streets,

Lord Have Mercy.
(A candle is extinguished.)

5) For the children in the world who are forced into the machinery and systems of warfare,

Lord Have Mercy.
(A candle is extinguished.)

6) For the teenagers who die each day from bullying, depression, and suicide,

Lord Have Mercy.
(A candle is extinguished.)

7) For the children who are lost to their families through rejection, kidnapping, and homelessness,

Lord Have Mercy.
(A candle is extinguished.)

8) For the not-quite-born surrendered to convenience, indifference, lack of desire,

Lord Have Mercy.
(A candle is extinguished.)

9) For the too-easily-forgotten, consumed by poverty,

Lord Have Mercy.
(A candle is extinguished.)

10) For the young ones whose lives will be cut short from alcohol and drug abuse,

Lord Have Mercy.
(A candle is extinguished.)

(Additional petitions can be added as needed. The litany ends with a period of silence.)

Let us pray:
Tender God, Lover of Us All: Like a mother who has lost her own children to senseless violence, You know the ways of humankind that so often destroy the innocent and the unprotected. Be with those around the globe—the mothers, the fathers, the families, the communities— who travel the path of grief and mourning. Sing with them their sorrowful songs until that day they are once again with those they love. We pray this together. Amen.

CLOSING SONG

"Sometimes I Feel Like a Motherless Child"

Sunday after Christmas

Feast of the Holy Family: A Prayer for Healing

BACKGROUND

The feast of the Holy Family draws our attention to the family of Jesus and their life together, stressing the virtues of a shared religious life as a model for all families. In Western Christianity, reverence for the Holy Family as a group arose in the seventeenth century (witness the many paintings done with the trio as subject matter), though in the East the theme was embraced earlier by the Coptic Church, due to the story of the flight into Egypt. The feast day was officially instituted by the Catholic Church in 1921, and in 1969 it was designated for the first Sunday after Christmas to blend it into the Christmas season.

APPLICATION

The nature of families has changed greatly from the exclusive description of the nuclear family. The realities of blended families, broken families, non-traditional families, and families-by-choice necessitate language and comprehension in pastoral or spiritual settings that are based on greater acceptance, understanding, and compassion. Rather than a prayer of praise or honor of Mary, Jesus, and Joseph, I have drafted a prayer focused on the healing of our families, where there is often so much turmoil and need.

SET UP

This can be prayed personally or communally, on this feast day or in other appropriate settings. Icons of the Holy Family may be placed with images of other families in an appropriate spot (altar, center of a circle, dining table, at a gravesite, etc.).

CALL TO PRAYER

We bring to mind the presence of God, the needs of the family (however it is being described), and the love of God. Attention may be drawn to photographs of families. When all are ready, the prayer begins.

Loving God
sweet, gilded images this holiday
   on Christmas cards,
glowing and moving words
   in letters about the families
   that are part of my history,
even TV ads about perfect
   gatherings around
   abundant tables
have reminded me that
   my family is not perfect,
   complete, or even whole.
I know that I am not alone.
I cannot name many people
   in my life whose families,
whatever their particular
   configuration may be,
are not touched by some
   wound, some altercation,
   some tragedy, some loss.
And so, contemplation of
   the Bethlehem trio of Jesus,
   Mary, and Joseph
can seem a little difficult,
   their image seeming distant
   and unreal.
It is not just the robes, the stars,
   or the angels in the corners
   of the house.
Word has it that they got along
   so impossibly well.
Their famous meekness
   and piety and love
   of one another
make my situation look really
   lame and a lot less than Holy.

The Winter Passage

So today, I am asking for
   the grace of healing
   in my family,
for like so many,
there are wounds in us,
   among us, old, new,
   gushing, scarred,
and we cannot, or will not,
   surrender to a healing hand.

I am asking for
   some open doors where
   there have been barriers,
carefully constructed, silently
   imposing, annoying,
   and constantly fortified.

I am inviting Your love,
   where there has been
   stubbornness
   and resentment:
we seem to have a gift for it—
unspoken words,
   clung-to stories of hurt,
   inability to forgive,
incapacity to forget or let go,
   landmines that keep us from
   moving on with one another.

We have trigger words
   that restart arguments,
internal buttons that,
   when pushed,
   inflame old battles,
well-rehearsed scripts of anger
   and self-justifications.

We have members that will not
   look or speak to one another,
and people who live in
   the same houses trapped
   in icy silences.

There are people I leave
   on hooks of guilt and blame,
and I have my own moments
   of shame and fear that leave
   me trapped.

I do believe You capable
   of miraculous things.
We don't need transformed
   water into wine,
but transformed hearts
   would be most welcome.

You need not liberate demons
   from among us,
unless they are the demons
   of our rage and old hurts.

None of us is leprous, but,
   beneath the skin,
   the scabs we pick at
are far from pretty
   and in need of staunch
   blood, new growth,
   and wholeness.

So, in this moment, before
   the New Year enters in,
let Mother Father Son
   and Daughter Sibling Grace
hasten from Bethlehem,
   a flight into another Egypt,
where I would ask You
   and Yours to take residence
and, day by day, in gentle ways,
   teach me and my family,
   my kin,
a different way to be together.

Amen.

∎ ∎ ∎

A Guided Meditation at New Year

A Prayer for Now

APPLICATION

New Year's Eve or Day gathering for home or church or community. This prayer form lends itself to a meditational setting that is not rushed. It could be part of a New Year's Eve prayer service that includes other elements like reviewing the year in the company of God, letting go of the past year's burdens, and so forth. This meditation could be done in the last hour of the old year or in the first hour of the new year. It could also be used as a centering call to prayer in a worship context.

SET UP

This is prayed by a group gathered in a quiet space. Candles or soft lighting are helpful. Extraneous noise or music are not. People should be able to sit comfortably, or possibly even lie down on the floor (while staying awake!).

CALL TO PRAYER

A leader gives an indication of the nature of the prayer and leads some simple deep breathing and some sort of call to mindfulness of God's presence in the community that is gathered. Or, if the group is formed in a circle, the parts of the prayer can go around the circle and be spoken by different readers. All take a deliberate breath between each line. The leader begins the prayer when all are ready.

This day You give me
God Beyond Time

This hour

This moment

This breath

This thought

Help me to be here

And nowhere else

With blessing
before me

Divine presence
within me

Eternal love
around me

Endless Light
shining through me

O God beyond
calendars and clocks
let me dwell often enough
in that realm
where there is only

NOW

in You

Help me to

Breathe in

And breathe out

The Winter Passage

Your Spirit
That I may find

My roots and wings
In You

Help me to embrace
the time that is mine

here and now

however long

or brief
Knowing that

All my time

Is enough

Is a gift

Is Yours

Give me grace enough

To live in the moment

To trust You always

To see You
In each encounter

To find You
In each person

To seek You
in every circumstance

To live well

All the time

You have given to me
NOW.

Amen.

■ ■ ■

A Service of Prayer and Reflection

At New Year: What to Do Now That the World Didn't End After All

APPLICATION

Around the New Year, for self, home, church, or community. This prayer form lends itself to a meditational setting that is not rushed. It could be part of a New Year mini-retreat with a variety of people or for one to make on one's own. Also works for the holiday in honor of Dr. Martin Luther King, Jr.

SET UP

This works well in a flexible space that allows for group prayer, private reflection/journal work, and some communal ritual. People should be able to sit comfortably. Candles or soft lighting are helpful, as is a source for meditational music during the writing. You need journals, pens, etc., or reflection booklets of some sort for writing (depending on time and resources, the reflection could be accomplished with magazine collage, watercolors, etc.). A tree branch (size depends on the size of the group) can be "planted" in some sturdy container or bucket in the center. Cut narrow strips of white paper and place them in a basket beneath the "tree" for the writing of blessings. Music (recorded or live) may be played at fitting parts of the prayer.

CALL TO PRAYER

A leader gives an indication of the nature of the prayer and then leads some simple centering and some sort of call to mindfulness of God's presence in the community that is gathered. If the group is formed in a circle, parts of the prayer can go around the circle and be spoken by different readers.

OPENING PRAYER

God beyond all names
   and times,
You who have made the world
   in all its mystery,
     who put life into humankind
        with its diverse gifts
        and possibilities,
draw us together, now,
   in this place, at the threshold
     of this new year.

We call to mind in this moment
   of beginning again,
people
   who have been shining
     examples
   of love and strength
     and courage,
     especially in this past year,
       (*We pause and remember.*)

events
that have led us from slavery
   into liberation,
from darkness into light,
and from violence into peace,
especially in this last year.
       (*We pause and remember.*)

We are grateful for traditions
   and paths
     that have led men and
        women to enlightenment.
     to the pursuit of what
        is true and beautiful,
     to generous service of others,
     and to knowledge of You.

We give thanks for Your abiding presence,
 Especially in this past year.
  (We pause and remember.)

As we face a new year together,
 may the power of our history
 and the assurance
  of Your presence
 help us
 to chose wisely,
 to live humbly,
 and to seek You in all the
  times and circumstances
   of this year as it unfolds.

This we pray together in
 Your Holy Name.
 Amen.

TIME FOR REFLECTION

(With appropriate materials for writing, drawing, etc., people are invited to engage in the quotes and questions below as they contemplate the coming year. Quiet music may be played in the background.)

"When you arise in the morning, think of what a precious privilege it is to be alive—to breathe, to think, to enjoy, to love." **Marcus Aurelius**

For Writing: What goals or aspirations do I imagine/plan for/intend/have for the coming year?

"I arise in the morning torn between a desire to improve the world and a desire to enjoy the world. This makes it hard to plan the day." **E. B. White**

"In dwelling, live close to the ground. In thinking, keep to the simple. In conflict, be fair and generous. In governing, don't try to control. In work, do what you enjoy. In family life, be completely present." **Lao Tzu**

For Writing: What upcoming challenges and opportunities do I face/encounter/engage/look forward to in this coming year?

"Do not dwell in the past, do not dream of the future, concentrate the mind on the present moment." **Buddha**

"If you enjoy living, it is not difficult to keep the sense of wonder." **Ray Bradbury**

For Writing: Where do I anticipate finding meaning in the coming months? How will I make meaning in the time ahead?

"When you dance, your purpose is not to get to a certain place on the floor. It's to enjoy each step along the way." **Wayne Dyer**

For Writing: Are there any departures/closures/changes ahead that will affect me?

(After being given sufficient time for the above, the group is invited to share, preferably in pairs, elements of the above. If the group is small, the sharing may happen in the larger group.)

(After enough time is given for sharing, the group is invited to participate in the litany below, with options for peoples' own intentions at the end of the litany. The petitions may be recited by a single leader or led by various people in the group.)

A SOLEMN LITANY OF PRAYER AT NEW YEAR

1) Let us pray for all believers.
 (Silence is kept; a chime may be rung.)
 Make us true to our calling,
  O God.
   **Give us the courage
    we need to live in truth.
   Give us the faith
    we need to follow You.
   Raise up leaders among us
    with new vision.
   Help us to serve others
    with generosity and joy.**

Hear our prayer, O God,
**May Your Spirit
make us new!**

2) Let us pray for our planet home, Earth.
(Silence is kept; a chime may be rung.)

Restore the work of Your hands, O God.
**Help us to be better
stewards of the planet.
Grant us the wisdom
and knowledge
to restore its waters.
Save us from the greed that
strips bare the lands.
Help us to heed the
warnings that are voiced
by all living things.**

Hear our prayer, O God,
**May Your Spirit
make us new!**

3) Let us pray for the communities of the world.
(Silence is kept; a chime may be rung.)

Restore Your people, O God.
**Grant us new ways to work
for the common good.
Give us a deeper regard
for the poor
and dispossessed.
Free us from greed and
the hunger for power.
Preserve us from deeds
born in fear and mistrust.**

**Help us to be patient
in every struggle
for justice.**

Hear our prayer, O God,
**May Your Spirit
make us new!**

4) Let us pray for the nation.
(Silence is kept; a chime may be rung.)

Renew the heart of our country, O God.
**Give us the grace to see our
faults and our strengths.
Free us from materialism,
selfishness, and fear.
Help us to live with
our differences
more gracefully.
Teach us to embrace those
who are poor
and homeless.
Help us all to seek
what is true.**

Hear our prayer, O God,
**May Your Spirit
make us new!**

5) Let us pray for this community. *(Silence is kept; a chime may be rung.)*

Make this a place of fruitfulness, generosity, and light.
**Give us joy in our work
with one another.
Free us from any bitterness
or misunderstanding.
Help us to grow in our gifts
and to reach out
to others.
Help us to grow in respect
and in compassion for
one another.
Bless our work in the
world, that it may lead to
Your Reign.**

Hear our prayer, O God,
**May Your Spirit
make us new!**

6) Let us pray for those who are sick. *(Silence is kept; a chime may be rung.)*

Hold those who need healing, O God:
**Those recovering
from illness,
Those who suffer
from addiction,
Those who suffer
from chronic pain
and disease,
And all who are dear to us
whom we remember now:**

(We remember in silence or aloud those who need healing.)

Hear our prayer, O God,
**May Your Spirit
make us new!**

7) Let us pray for those who have died. *(Silence is kept; a chime may be rung.)*

Bring us all to eternal life, O God:

The Winter Passage

**Those who have died alone,
or imprisoned,
Those who have died
by violence, warfare,
or neglect,
Those who have died
forgotten or abandoned,
And all who are dear to us
whom we remember
now:**

(We remember in silence or aloud those who have died.)

Hear our prayer, O God,
**May Your Spirit
make us new!**

8) Are there other prayers of this community?

(Time is left for prayers from the people. At the end of the prayer a leader continues.)

LEADER:
Hear the prayer of all Your people, O God, for this day and for the year to come.
**May the lifting of our
hearts and minds to You
lead us to action.
Increase our faith
and deepen our trust.**

Throughout the time to come that is granted us, may You lead us in peace. Lead us, and those we meet, to blessing.
**May the life we share here
honor You and give witness
to Your presence in our age.**
We pray together. **AMEN.**

THE WRITING OF THE BLESSINGS

(What blessing(s) do you need for this new year? What help or grace to be the person God invites you to be?

We write on the narrow white papers [tied with narrow white ribbon or string] the blessing we ask for the year. People may use as many strips as they like.)

HANGING OF THE BLESSINGS

(As we finish writing the blessings we seek for this year, we hang them on the branches of the tree. The tree remains in a viewable space for a period of time. At the beginning of the season of Lent, the blessings could be put into a vessel and kept in a special place for the year.)

A CLOSING PRAYER

Lover of the Human Soul,
for this new year born
mysteriously of night's
turning into day,
we give thanks.
Open our ears
to hear the words we need
to hear in the days
and months to come,
even when they
are hard words.
Open our hearts
to keep the words we need
to keep,
even when they are heavy,
challenging words.
Open our minds
to act on the words
that are spoken,
especially when they lead us
to justice.
Open our spirits
to receive the words
that are spoken,
especially when we are
discouraged and afraid.
Open our mouths
to speak the truth that is
given to each of us,
especially when it leads
others to freedom.
AMEN.

A BLESSING

O Holy One,
Abide with us
In this hour,
In our rest,
In all the time that is ours
in the year to come.
Let your blessing rest
Upon us, within us, around us
in this moment and in
all the moments to come.
In Your name we pray. **AMEN.**

■ ■ ■

An Epiphany—New Year Night

Blessing From the Four Directions

APPLICATION

With its archetypal structure in facing the four cardinal directions, this prayer is well suited to a New Year's gathering with some degree of formality. It's fitting for home or church or community and is ecumenical in its essence. This prayer form lends itself to the use of a wide range of images and symbols. It can stand on its own or could be an opening for a larger New Year's prayer service, retreat, or a call to prayer for a liturgy.

SET UP

This is prayed by a group gathered in a space where people can physically turn north, south, east, west, and to a physical center of the room (a circle formation is helpful). Candles or other symbolic objects (scented oil, incense, etc.) are helpful but not mandatory, and their use indicated below is only one possibility. This could be prayed in the light of the Christmas tree at night (or pre-dawn) or in the full light of morning.

CALL TO PRAYER

A leader gives an indication of the nature of the prayer and gives a call to mindfulness of God's presence and grace that comes to us from all around. There could be some recollection of time past or an opening to the time yet to be experienced.

The leader begins the prayer when all are ready. Designated readers pray each of the directions. Additional people may help with the actions. All read the parts in bold.

1. (*We turn to the east, where a tall, white candle is lit.*)

Creator of the Universe, in this long season of timeless dark, we celebrate Your Light dawning in our world.

In these weeks where nights grow gradually shorter, we bless You for the slow turn of our planet that sets the sun rising higher in the sky. We praise You for the return of this longed-for light and the promise of a spring for our hard and brittle hearts.

We remember the marvelous fire that drew wise men and women to a hay-strewn cave, where the distance between heaven and earth was shattered forever as the shining Son arose.

**At the East Gate of the year,
We bless You and we call:
Shine upon us,
   Creator God!**

(*We light our individual tapers from the large candle.*)

---

2. (*We turn to the south, where sticks of incense are lit and placed in a brass pot of sand.*)

Giver of the Gifts of Life, we bless You for the air that surrounds us and the breath we take. We bless You for the fire in our blood and the pulsing in our veins.

We recall the journey and

The Winter Passage

dreams of the Magi, with their gifts of royal gold, fragrant frankincense, and the balm of soothing myrrh. We thank You for the Wanderers' wonder and longing, which we share.

We praise You for journeys we each make to find You. We recall the gifts of Earth that remind us of the holy life and nobility that Christ shares with us along the way.

At the South Gate of the year, We bless you and we call: Make us truly holy, Spirit God.

(We anoint one another's foreheads with scented oil from a number of small bowls that are brought out by helpers.)

---

3. *(We turn to the west, where a festive holiday bread is broken into many pieces [if the group is large, some of this can be accomplished before the service].)*

Lover of the Human Soul, with Jesus who shared our bread, our needs, and our rugged ways, we celebrate the feast begun in Bethlehem's hearth.

We recall with awe and gratitude the tender ways in which he fed Your people, born of a world that clings to its hunger. We give thanks for his generous spirit that made its home at the tables of the rich, the poor, the proud, and the humble.

With the shepherds and kings and the mothers and babes of Ancient Bethlehem, we rejoice in the Word made flesh, and the Hope made known, and the Banquet of Love made real in our midst.

At the West Gate of the year, We bless You and we call: Feed and nourish us, Creator God.

(We share a taste of the festive bread passed around the circle or brought out by helpers.)

---

4. *(We turn to the north, where a festive drink [wine/juice] is poured out into one or several cups, depending on the size of the group.)*

Holy One, Maker of Earth and all within it, we are humbled by the planet's beauty and recall that which sustains and nourishes us in Your Creation.

We give thanks for the Child of Heaven and the Child of Earth, who offered light to a people that loved its blindness, and extended the Great Invitation to people afraid to hear its own true name.

We bless You that Jesus, from beginning to end, poured out his life, in all its richness, and embraced our Death, in all its mystery. We praise You for his rising in our midst so that we might know the fullness of Life.

At the North Gate of the year, We bless You and we call: Make us truly human, Creator God.

(We share a taste of the festive drink.)

---

5. At this festival time, at the beginning of possibilities, we celebrate the richness of our lives, O God, and we rejoice.

We praise You for the invitation to Your great banquet, where the filled and the wanting, the healthy and the unwhole, and the restless and the homed sit side by side.

At this winter festival of stars and wonder and gifts and journeys, of new lights and ancient darks, we bless You.

At every portal of this year All Your people praise and call: Be with and bless and burn within, Creating, Saving God. AMEN.

(Music begins. We light votive candles and take them all over the building, at every door and window. And, perhaps, we feast.)

■ ■ ■

A Table Prayer

For the Epiphany Season

APPLICATION

At Epiphany or beyond, this prayer is for home or church or community use. Suitable for a parish meeting, family gathering, retreat, ecumenical gathering of several communities, etc. This prayer form lends itself to a potluck. It borrows some of the elements of the Epiphany Blessing From the Four Directions, and is constructed for a gathering around a table (an *Agape*), although in some circumstances it can be adapted for a great thanksgiving in liturgical settings.

SET UP

This is prayed by a group gathered around a single (expanded) table or at a series of tables. Tables can be set as simply or as elaborately as resources allow. Candlelight and tablecloths are conducive to the sense of a ceremonial meal. Plenty of candles, perhaps amidst star garlands or ornaments, can help underscore the festival nature of the ceremony.

At the table, all have a copy of the text and a glass. The fruit of the vine (wine or juice) is distributed to each person's glass before the prayer. A loaf of bread (perhaps a sweet holiday loaf that has rich cinnamon or other spices) for breaking is in readiness at a leader's place, or loaves of bread can be present at each table.

Individuals read the numbered portions. (This can be designated in advanced or done spontaneously.) All read the parts in bold.

CALL TO PRAYER

The meal begins with an indication of the nature of the prayer and some sort of call to mindfulness (quiet, intentional breathing or meditational music or a song). A designated leader lights a candle and begins the prayer when all are ready.

1) Creator of the Universe, in this long season of timeless dark, we celebrate Your Light dawning in our world.

2) As nights grow ever shorter, we bless You for the slow turning of our planet that sets the sun rising higher in the sky.

3) We praise You for the return of this longed-for light, the promise of spring for our hard and brittle earth, and, even now, for the slow growing of things, nearly unperceived.

**In a time of darkness and change,
we bless You, and we ask You:
Be light within us, Loving God!**

4) Creator of the great night sky, we bless You for dark, for shadows, and for midnight stillness, within us and around us.

5) We remember that Holy Night, and we recall with joy the great star that announced the coming of Your Son's light into our world.

6) We call to mind that onetime fire that drew men and women to a hay-strewn place, where the distance between heaven and earth was shattered forever.

**In a time of winter dark and stars,
we bless You, and we ask You:
Shine upon us, Living God!**

7) Lover of the Human Soul, we recollect those ways Your Christ was announced within our world, the witness of John the Baptizer, the enthusiastic response of those who came to first follow Jesus, the Good News unfolding to Your Chosen people, and beyond.

The Winter Passage

8) We know that we too share in the witness, the call, the response, and a life of faith that is shared with people from around the world throughout time.

9) We recall with awe and gratitude the ways in which Jesus shone in a world that loved its blindness and issued Your call to a people afraid to hear its true name.

> **In a time of faith and challenge,
> we bless You and ask You:
> Be Fire within us, Holy God!**

10) Giver of the Gifts of Life, we bless You for the breath we take and for the pulsing of the blood in our veins.

11) With Jesus, who shared our rugged ways, we praise You for the mystery of our lives and even for our dying.

12) At this table we celebrate the richness of life and praise You for the invitation to Your royal banquet, where kings and beggars sit side by side.

> **At this table of many graces,
> we bless You, and we ask You:
> Feed and nourish us, Tender God!**

(We raise the bread and the leader says:)

With the gift of the grain, born of the earth, and fashioned by human hands:

> **We Bless You, God, Most High!**

(We pass the bread, break off a piece, and eat. When all have eaten, we raise our glasses, and the leader says:)

With the gift of the vine, born of the earth and fashioned by human hands:

> **We Bless You, God, Most High!**

(We drink the fruit of the vine.)

13) With ancient witnesses named and unnamed, with brothers and sisters known and unknown, with shepherds and kings, and the mothers and babes of long-ago Bethlehem, with the Baptizer, and the disciples, and the witnesses throughout the ages,

> **we rejoice in the Word-Made-Flesh,
> and the Love-Made-Known,
> and the Hope-Made-Real,
> here, now, in our midst,
> at this table, with this feast,
> we bless You, and we ask:
> Make us truly human, Creator God!**

14) Through and with Jesus Your Son, our Brother and Lord, we pray together.
Amen.

(Instructions may be given for potluck or other meal, or this concluding prayer below may be recited by a leader. This prayer can also be used at the end of the potluck.)

O God, Great Mystery and Sustainer of our lives,
we know You better
when we share with one another
our daily bread and the drink
that delights and nourishes us.

May our simple feast of bread and wine keep us
aware of all that sustains us
each day in our lives,
both food and companionship,
both drink and Presence.

We bless You at this table and all the tables of our lives, and we ask Your blessing as we go forth from this place to continue our Advent Journey. **Amen.**

Let us go in peace. **Thanks be to God.**

∎ ∎ ∎

AT THE BAPTISM OF JESUS

A Water Prayer

APPLICATION

At or around the feast of the Baptism of Jesus (the Orthodox celebration of Epiphany), at New Year, for a creation prayer or an environment service or another suitable time of blessing or beyond. This prayer is for home or church or community use. It can be adapted for retreats, an ecumenical gathering of several communities, etc.

SET UP

This ceremony requires various vessels for pouring, sprinkling, and containing water (as indicated in directions below). Care can be taken to find beautiful vessels, but makeshift vessels will do as well. This might be prayed outdoors in a variety of settings as well as in a ceremonial space. The opening invocation, "Let Your Healing Fall On Us Like Rain," can be set to music or gestured without music.

CALL TO PRAYER

The ritual prayer begins with an indication of the nature of the prayer and some sort of call to mindfulness (quiet, intentional breathing or meditational music or a song). As part of the beginning of the prayer, a designated leader may offer the introduction as written or ad-lib.

INTRODUCTION

Water has been a significant and repeated factor in the injuries sustained by our global body in recent times. From the catastrophic ruin of the Asian tsunami to the damage of multiple hurricanes and the enduring devastation of broken levees in New Orleans, we see full well the destructive powers of water.

The abiding tragedy of the absence of drinkable water in parts of Africa, Asia, and South America only occasionally enters our consciousness as a nation but nevertheless remains a scandal. Our own ongoing struggle with pollution in seas and waterways reminds us of how precarious a time it is for creation and for the water that gives it life and form.

In drought-affected parts of the United States, with its desert-like winters, people experience in their dry skin, bloody noses, and scratchy eyes the daily reality of our need for water. Our bottled, designer water is as ubiquitous as our cell phones. Most of us feel acutely our intimate need for water. We may even be among those who pray for some portion of the rains that fall, seemingly non-stop, in other parts of the country.

Today, in praying for blessing, we turn to the positive power of water—as a natural force and as a symbol. With its capacity to move and change, its ability to heal and restore, its gift to bring life into the desert and hope to the prairie, it is a potent image for the kind of healing that we might ask for as individuals, as a community, and as a nation. Our various sacred writings celebrate the restorative powers of rain in parched lands and tell of mercy that falls freely from the heavens. Today, let us be open to that same outpouring.

Please remain seated as we begin our ceremony with an invocation.

INVOCATION

(Spoken/danced with congregational antiphon [gestured and spoken or sung];

Leader introduces and teaches refrain.)

Let your healing fall like rain upon us.

Speaker 1:
God our Maker,
The world you have created
is bruised with our careless
    use of resources.
The wounds we inflict upon
    our planet home grow
    deeper every day.
The growing things cry out;
    we shut our ears.
The living things disappear;
    we close our eyes.
The skies grow dark
    with the sins of our excess.

Stretch out Your hand
    and lead us
Out of the desert
    of our mindless living.

Let your healing fall like rain upon us.

Speaker 2:
God our Source,
The people you have
    brought into being
are torn by prejudice, poverty,
    and warfare.
The wounds we inflict on
    one another grow deeper
    every day.
The poor cry out;
    we shut our ears.
The homeless multiply daily;
    we close our eyes.
Famine and disease spread
    like wildfire.
The graves of children mark
    the sins of our excess.

Stretch out Your hand
    and lead us
Out of the desert
    of our careless living.

Let your healing fall like rain upon us.

Speaker 3:
God our Lover,
The people you have called
    into faith
are embattled by difference
    and misunderstanding.
The wounds we inflict
    in Your name grow deeper
    every day.
The people at the margins
    cry out; we shut our ears.
The widow and the orphan
    challenge us; we close
    our eyes.
Our fear of one another
    makes us enemies in faith.
The wars of religions mark
    the sins of our
    hardened hearts.

Stretch out Your hand
    and lead us
Out of the desert
    of self-righteous living.

Let your healing fall like rain upon us.

Speaker 4:
God our Foundation,
This community You have
    brought into being
is not always what
    we hope to be.
The wounds we inflict on
    one another are real.
We shut our ears to one another.
We close our eyes to
    opportunities to change,
    to grow.

We are not always mindful
   of how we are called.
We often ignore the vocations
   that make us unique.

Stretch out Your hand
   and lead us
Out of the desert of our living
   less than we might be.

**Let your healing fall
like rain upon us.**

PRAYER

God Most High, Spirit most
   deep, be with us this day
and rain down on the parts of us
that are hardened by
fear, indifference, ignorance,
   or hate.

Wash away all that blinds
   or binds us.
Renew what needs
   to be restored.
Bring us to new life in You.

For we pray to You in
   many ways, in many names,
And You love us all.
   God forever and ever. **Amen.**

COLLECTING OF
THE WATERS OF OUR NEEDS

(People bring small containers of water from the large containers in the back or perimeter of the space.

As they are poured into a main vessel, we name our cares, needs for healing, concerns of our world, needs specific to time, place, community, etc.)

THE GREAT OUTPOURING

Leader introduces:
We pour vessels of water into
the large bowl to symbolize
the resources within our
community:

(Speakers read the narrative as water is poured. There is instrumental background music throughout [e.g., "Peace is Flowing Like A River"].)

Waters of Birth:

We bring the waters of birth—
with death, the most common
   of human experiences.

Water is the air we breathe for
   nine months in the womb,
swimming and hiccupping
   in this sacred pool
until it breaks, gushes,
   and spills out new life.

Never to return to this safe
   sacred place,
the newborn lets out a wail
   and gasps for breath.
Soap and water cleanse
   away blood.
As breast milk flows,
the infant desperately suckles
away as though
life depends upon it,
and it does.
A refreshing drink replenishes
   the new mother's strength,
and the cycle of life goes on.
We pour the water of these
   universal rites of initiation
that 300,000 women will
   undergo today,
      and tomorrow,
and the day after that.

Waters of Knowledge
and Learning:

We bring the waters
   of knowledge and
      comprehension.

Since ancient times, water
   has been a symbol
      for knowledge.
The Greeks saw Aquarius bearing
   the waters of knowledge
      through the heavens.
Eastern traditions sought
   wisdom to slake the thirst
      of searching minds.
The fount of knowledge
   is a common image in the
      human quest to improve.
Without knowledge, our minds
   are small and uncaring,
our hearts dry and sterile.

Only with learning will seeds
   of wisdom and compassion
take root within us
   and burst forth in full flower.

The Winter Passage

We learn to open our minds
   and hearts;
We learn to change
   our communities;
We learn to work for
   a better world.

We pour the waters
   of knowledge and learning
that help us transform this
world into a garden of peace.

Waters of Diversity:

We bring the water of diversity,
the unifying force of who
   we are and hope to become.

We bathe in the diversity
   of heritages,
each worthy of celebration,
which strengthen our
   communities and families.

We swim in a sea of many types
   and shapes and colors,
creatures of such beauty
   and ability,
all signs in their distinctiveness
of a Creator in love with
   complexity and variety.

We draw strength from
   the diversity of our spiritual
   journeys
that come together
   by many names
in this time and this place
to bless the work that is
   entrusted to us.

We pour this water that moves
   through us as one body
created from the unique gifts
   of its individual parts.

Waters of Our Traditions and Stories:

We bring the water of
   the traditions and stories
     that make us who we are.

Our ancestors have carried
   the stories of who we are
   for generations:
the journeys and struggles
   of our families,
the present challenges of us
   and our children
our new links with new people
   increase the possibilities
     of who we are becoming.

We bring the living water
   of our various identities
     and experiences,
our understandings
   of the human thirst for God,
our traditions that water
   our souls,
the wisdom that flows
   from so many lives,
and the waves of inspiration that
   travel through our people.
We pour the water of centuries
   of becoming tradition
that renews and nurtures
   our communities today.

Waters of Healing:

We bring waters of healing:
traditions and ways of tending
   to the body and soul in need.

We bring efforts of
   the seasoned among us,
years of learning from
   life's challenges,
wisdom gained from mastering
   the art of living to the full.

We bring the enthusiasm
   and energy of the young
     among us,
the vitality and hope they bring
   from Life's newness,
the eagerness for others
   to follow their lead.

We bring gifts of healing:
the touch of a beloved's hand,
a source of hope to a heart
   of suffering;
the encouragement
   of a parent's voice,
coaxing patience in
   the healing process,
the insights, intuitions, and
   knowledge of caregivers;
the tenacity and compassion
to nourish life,
and the wisdom to ease the way
   toward death,
the prayers and community
   that support healing arts.

We bring the gifts of listening,
the capacity to hold
	another's story,
the grace to know when
	to speak and when
		to keep silence,
the power to release
	and to forgive,
the courage to seek forgiveness.

We bring the waters of healing.

BLESSING OF WATERS

*(A leader or participant,
with hands outstretched over
the bowl of gathered water, says:)*

God our Creator
in ageless Time,
Your Spirit moved over
	the waters
and brought life to our planet.

Let that Spirit move over
	these waters today,
the waters of our needs
	and of our riches,
the waters that are the source
	of our healing
as a world, as a community.

Move on these waters,
	and move among us
with blessing and with healing.
Restore us in Your endless love.

Amen.

SPRINKLING OF THE CONGREGATION

(Designated persons [or volunteers] take up pine or leafy branches from around the bowl. They dip them into the water in the bowl, and head into the congregation, sprinkling the people. There is music during the sprinkling.)

CLOSING BLESSING

A Leader or other:

Gracious God,
May we truly experience
	Your Life-Giving waters!

May we drink satisfaction
	of right relationships in our
		personal and professional
			lives.
May our ears hear oceans
	of healing and restoration
		in our lives and around
			the world.
May we use our hands
	as an extension of Your love
to carry drafts of Your love
	to thirsty neighbors near
		and far.
May our eyes be cleared
	to see Your world reorient
		around tides of love.
May the moisture of Your peace
	and justice refresh our hearts
		and minds.

This Blessing we ask
	through Your Spirit
as we acknowledge our role
	in this creative work.

Amen.

■ ■ ■

The Winter Passage

Rev. Martin Luther King, Jr.

Holiday Prayer Service

BACKGROUND

A holiday honoring the life and work of Dr. Martin Luther King, Junior, was first signed into law in 1983, although actual observance didn't take place until three years later. Many states and communities resisted the creation of this federal holiday (near the January 15 birthday of the slain civil rights leader). It wasn't until the year 2000 that all 50 states actually observed it. With its remembrances of his profound oratory and history-altering, nonviolent action, Martin Luther King Day has become an event that reminds us of the courage and power of the preacher who transformed the course of civil rights in America, and likewise indicates how much further there is to go.

APPLICATION

The prayer below is an invitation to consider the legendary "dream" of Dr. King and the necessity to move beyond words and nostalgia. Suitable for many community situations, it is open to additions and editing.

SET UP

This can be prayed personally or communally, on or near the holiday. Fitting in churches, civic settings, or schools, it lends itself to interfaith participation. Images of Dr. King can be inspiring; a source of light and flame reminiscent of the burning bush of Exodus can be helpful, depending on the setting. There are an appropriate numbers of bowls of oil (olive oil, scented with essential oils) for the anointing.

CALL TO PRAYER

We bring to mind the presence of God, the needs of our nation to continue the work enacted by Dr. King, and the need to make this work a part of our own lives and not just a historical remembrance. When all are ready, the prayer begins.

OPENING PRAYER

God of all Creation,
   as a people of faith,
our history over the ages
   is a story filled with
   Your saving power,
Your boundless love,
   Your dream for all
   the human family.

You desire to lead us out
   of slavery of every kind:
   Our devotion to greed
     and acquisition,
   Our relentless hunger
     for power,
   Our constant blindness
     to brothers and sisters
     in need.

As we gather together
   before You today,
we remember that You raise up
   human beings to speak
   words that rouse the weary
   and anger the powerful.

   You lead men and women to
challenge what is,
   and put forth the dream of
what may be.

Your Spirit raises up courage
   in the weak,
   and comforts the afflicted.

May that same Spirit
   be with us today so that
   Your dream

of genuine freedom
may be reborn in us,
    so that Your prophetic power
    may find a voice in us,
so that Your Vision for
    all people may find a home
    in our words and actions.

For that same Spirit gives us
    the courage to call out
    to You,
Source of Life, now and forever,
Amen.

A READING FROM THE BOOK OF EXODUS

Exodus 3:1–2

Moses was tending the flock of his father-in-law Jethro, the priest of Midian. Leading the flock across the desert, he came to Horeb, the mountain of God. Then an angel of the Lord appeared to him in fire flaming out of a bush. As he looked on, he was surprised to see that the bush, though on fire, was not consumed. So Moses decided, I must go over to look at this remarkable sight, and see why the bush is not burned.

When the Lord saw him coming over to look at it more closely, God called out to him from the bush, "Moses! Moses!" He answered, "Here I am." God said, "Come no nearer! Remove the sandals from your feet, for the place where you stand is holy ground. I am the God of your father," He continued, "the God of Abraham, the God of Isaac, the God of Jacob." Moses hid his face, for he was afraid to look at God. "So indeed the cry of the Israelites has reached me, and I have truly noted that the Egyptians are oppressing them. Come, now! I will send you to Pharaoh to lead my people, the Israelites, out of Egypt."

But Moses said to God, "Who am I that I should go to Pharaoh and lead the Israelites out of Egypt?" He answered, "I will be with you; and this shall be your proof that it is I who have sent you: when you bring my people out of Egypt, you will worship God on this very mountain."

Hear what the Spirit is saying to the people!

Thanks Be to God!

REFLECTION AND SHARING

(In a few moments of quiet, we reflect on the following. Writing responses may be useful, or this can be done as a guided reflection.)

Do I feel there is a "burning bush" in my life? Something that may both draw me and cause me trepidation? An issue or circumstance that requires intervention?

Whom do I see as captive? Where do I feel led to speak out or to act on behalf of others? To what situations might I help bring peace? What grace or strength do I need?

What keeps me from taking action for those "held captive"?

(Depending on the time and setting, people may share their reflections with one another.)

WORDS OF REFLECTION

(Someone may be invited to share insights about the day and the theme of the prayer, or the above may be processed in a larger group.)

A LITANY OF THE PEOPLE

(Different people may call out the petitions as numbered from the group, or selected people may read the statements below from a lectern or other space. The response is after each statement. All speak the portions in bold type.)

1) O God, they mock me

The Winter Passage

because my skin is black.
They see me as meant for slavery
    and prone to crime.
They look at me with fearful
    hearts and see me not at all.
Hear Your People.

Set us free!

2) O God, they keep me
    from the job I can do
    because my skin is brown.
They laugh at me and call me
    "illegal" and "fence hopper."
They judge me
    with bitter hearts,
    but know me not at all.
Hear Your People.

Set us free!

3) O God, they say my poverty
    is my own choice.
Their schools are places for
    the privileged and the rich.
They lock me from their world
    and call it just.
Hear Your People.

Set us free!

4) O God, they say I am
    a woman and belong at home.
Their angry judgments
    and unfeeling hearts
    condemn my family.
How do I feed my children
    without a job?
Hear Your People.

Set us free!

**Set us free, O saving God.
Give us eyes to see and ears
    to hear.
Break our stony hearts
    and open our
        shuttered minds.
Open us to Your dream
    for us!**

5) O God, they beat me bleeding
    and hang me on a fence to die.
They call me "faggot" and "queer."
They use Your name to justify
    their violent acts.
Hear Your People.

Set us free!

6) O God, I am the child
    of ancient hates and bigotry.
I struggle to live in
    a different way and fail.
It's hard to go against the way
    I was raised.
Hear Your People.

Set us free!

7) O God, I curse Your way
    and Your weak-minded fools.
Hate is the fire that burns
    in me and makes me blind.
It's my world. I am supreme.
    My color, my sex, my money,
    makes me so.
Hear Your People.

Set us free!

8) O God, we've tried for years
    to make changes
    in our world.
We are more at odds with
    one another than ever before.
I'm too tired to try anymore.
    I'm too discouraged.

**Set us free, O saving God.
Give us eyes to see and ears
    to hear.
Break our stony hearts
    and open our
        shuttered minds.
Open us to Your dream
    for us!**

9) O God, I don't know
    what the fuss is all about.
I'm not prejudiced. There aren't
    any really big problems.
Why do people think things
    need to change?
Hear Your People.

Set us free!

AN ANOINTING FOR ACTION

Leader: In Biblical times, and through the present day throughout the Church, people have been anointed with oil for many reasons, including healing, blessing, and assignment to a specific task or ministry.

Today we will anoint one another with oil to recall that we each are invited to actively bring forth the Reign of God's justice and compassion, in our own ways, in our given circumstances, with the particular gifts that we have been given.

As we anoint one another's upturned palms with the scented oil, I invite you to say to each other:

May Your gifts bring freedom to others.

to which you can respond:

Let it be so!

(We anoint one another with the oil. Appropriate music may accompany the blessing.)

A BLESSING

(One or several readers may be engaged for the following.)

Leader: As we prepare to go into the world and be a people of thinking and action, we ask for God's blessing in the spirit of Dr. King.

Prophetic voices call us to live beyond the confines of our slavish individuality and in solidarity with the experience of other lives.

Let us be a people of deeper living!

We are called to look beyond the shadowy monuments of disappointment into the day when all share in freedom's legacies.

Let us be a people of hope!

We are called to have hearts and minds that strive to comprehend the struggle of others.

Let us be a people of compassion!

The work to which we are called requires a change of systems, patterns, and long-lived habits; it requires time!

Let us be a people of patience!

The work to which we are called requires the brave examination of our own words, tendencies, shadows, and shortcomings.

Let us be a people who can change!

The work to which we are called requires imagination, creativity, ingenuity, and new vision.

Let us be a people who dream!

A FINAL BLESSING

And May God bless us all in the journey ahead:

God who has created us,

God who sets us free,

God who inspires us to act for others.

Amen.

THE DISMISSAL

Let us go forth in courage and strength,
to be a people of action and peace,
wherever we live, work, and learn.

Amen.

■ ■ ■

Mozart's Birthday

In Gratitude for Music Makers

BACKGROUND

Wolfgang Amadeus Mozart (January 27, 1756 – December 5, 1791) was one of the most prolific composers of the Classical Period of Western music. A child prodigy, he was carted around the courts of Europe to play for the heads of state of numerous countries. He produced over 600 pieces of orchestral, choral, symphonic, and operatic work and had a profound effect on future composers (such as Beethoven). His ecclesiastical music is especially inspiring. His music is characterized by great vitality, energy, and no little joy.

Despite his prolific output and popularity, Mozart had a hard time achieving financial stability for himself and his family. He died poor. His work was popularized globally in the years after his death.

APPLICATION

The prayer below is an invitation to be aware of gifted composers like Mozart and to be thankful for musicians and composers who add such quality to our lives. The prayer can be adapted for other musicians, including musicians in one's own community.

SET UP

This prayer can be prayed in a variety of settings but is ideal in a communal situation where music is a bond or agency for worship.

INTRODUCTION/ WELCOME

(Someone indicates the composer's birth and notable accomplishments.)

WE READ

Psalm 150

Hallelujah!
Praise! Praise God in the temple,
   in the highest heavens!
Praise! Praise God's mighty deeds
   and noble majesty.
Praise! Praise God with trumpet
   blasts with lute and harp
Praise! Praise God with timbrel
   and dance, with strings
   and pipes.
Praise! Praise God with
   crashing cymbals,
   with ringing cymbals.
Let all that has life and breath,
   praise. Praise God,
      Hallelujah!

WE LISTEN

Mozart's "Exsultate, Jubilate"

"Rejoice, shout, O you blessed souls, singing sweet hymns; responding to your song the skies sing psalms with me."

WE REFLECT

Recall a time you were transported, transfixed, or transformed by a piece of music. What was it and what happened?

What music moves you the most to consider the divine? When?

What is it that is so distinctive about music and the movement of your spirit or soul?

What makes sharing about music so engaging?

WE SHARE

(Discussion is based on the questions above.)

WE PRAY

A Blessing for Musicians

Almighty God, from the beginning, You have been the Creator of beautiful and marvelous sounds, sounds that inspire, delight, and even terrify Your creatures. And as You have poured out the music of Your Holy Spirit to bring life to human beings, You poured out some of that same sound of Your very self, who are imaged in human flesh.

We ask Your blessing today upon musical artists whose work is holy work, indeed. They bring to life the songs of the soul, the intimations of the heavens, the utterances of sorrow, and the exultations of joy. We give thanks for song and music that inspires, gives hope, uplifts the tired heart, and makes joy in so many lives.

Bless the music makers, their hands, their brains, their voices, and their ability to make material come alive. May they be always fruitful in their work their whole lives long.

(The leader invites the people to finish the prayer with him/her.)

O Creating God, we thank You for the gifts of all musicians—instrumentalists, singers, and composers—all people who respond to You with courage, faith, and creativity. They reflect the beauty of Your many works and tell the great and simple stories of the human experience, throughout every age. They express what simple words cannot. They are a powerful and essential gift to the human family.

Thank You for musical artists among us and all the musicians whose work we celebrate and enjoy. May they continue to create many works that praise You, inspire their listeners, and give them joy as creative people. We pray through the power of Your always-creating Spirit.

Amen.

■ ■ ■

Meditation after Yuletide

Holiday In and Out and Onward

People laugh at me.
It's January, almost February,
My Christmas trees
    are just coming down
(Yes, "trees." I'm a man of excess.
If one is good, eight
    must be better).

Groundhogs and Cupid
    are waiting at the door,
My home is stripping
    for ordinary time.

In the living room,
a solitary Saint Nicholas
(on a gold and fragile globe)
presides from piney treetop
(fake, enduring, safe)
over a landscape
    of naked branches
(skeletal with colored lights
    still blazing)
and boxes
(ready for stuffing
    and basement oblivion).
Piles of tender glory
(just out of dog's reach)
await tedious ceremonies
    of storage.

A necessary paring down,
not quite Lenten,
but after gold and glass
    and glitz,
it's austere, and welcome,
    in its way.

This is a job I do slowly,
    reluctantly
(procrastination my shield).
When resolve reaches
    critical mass
I wrap, and roll, and stuff,
    and tote,
pondering my sin
    of acquisition and
the space
that emerges finally out
    of too-full finery.

I breathe.

As welcome as Yuletide was,
its surface remnants remind me
of the incarnations that didn't
quite
take
this year.

It wasn't the brown Christmas:
red-rimmed epistles unsent,
family unseen,
imperfect music played brief,
or any want of taste or touch.

Amidst the wreckage
    and the wrapping,
despite nativities
    from three countries,
cut glass dishes shining with
chocolate, figs, pistachio,
    peppermint,
resplendent wreaths
    near-choked
with glassy clusters like grapes,
iterations of Santa Claus
    of every ethnic sway,
angel hosts in wood, plaster,
    plastic, clay,
tin hearts and tiny toys,
I sense that Jesus
    went under-fleshed.

Though no little effort
    went to making house
Martha-Stewart-ready
and American-Greetings-proud,
some homemaking
    was neglected nonetheless,
and my forest of faux pine
    cannot hide me.
Thin gold and molded fantasies
    do nothing
to buffer the post-Christmas
    rebuke.

So,
boxing all beauty away
    for another year,
naked space blesses me,
and reminds me of
    the naked place within,
ready
(still)
for Christ-clothing.

In honest plainsong,
    the unadorned
table,
chair,
hearth,
wall,
sing their humble,
    hopeful hymn of everyday,
no matter gathered dust,
neglected mail.
The Coming that counts
    is before me still.
A Magi journey's just begun,
starless,

but real.

■ ■ ■

Part III
Winter into Spring

Prayer Service
At the Quickening of the Year

BACKGROUND

Most people, especially in winter-ravaged areas, are conscious of the first of the spring-approaching "feasts"—that of Groundhog Day. We hungrily await the lengthening of days, the cracking of ice in bodies of water, and the revelation of things growing through the still-very-cold earth. Like many of our Western days of observance, February 2 is connected to the Celtic (and agrarian) calendar, through the festival of Imbolc ("in milk"), which celebrates the first stirrings of spring from the depths of winter. Farm animals begin to lactate (to prepare for new life), the first buds emerge on trees, daylight is visibly longer, and temperatures begin to relent in their fierceness. The Celtic festival, with its devotion to the goddess Brid, became Christianized as the feast of Saint Brigid. It is also known as the feast of the Presentation of Jesus in the Temple, and Candlemas, when candles for church use through the year would be blessed.

APPLICATION

At or around February 2, for self, home, church, or community. This prayer service lends itself to observation of the slow shift of seasons. It could be part of an afternoon or evening of reflection with a variety of people or used on one's own as an extended meditation. Most parts can be used as separate elements.

SET-UP

Any reflective space may be used; one that allows manipulation of light (dark to light) is helpful. Writing materials are useful (reflection questions can also be "answered" more creatively with collage, painting, or drawing supplies). Reflection questions can be shared if time, space, and circumstance allow. Prayer/reflection can begin with a brief explanation of the significance of the time/season and a simple centering.

CALL TO PRAYER

(Lights are dimmed or off. This reflection can be done in writing or as a spoken, guided meditation.)

In what season do I find myself these days?

What are the outer manifestations of that season?

What are the inner movements or signs of that season?

What are the changes I feel happening in me? Within the circles of my life?

Have I been here before?

(OPTION FOR SHARING OR SITTING IN THE QUIET)

(OPTION FOR APPROPRIATE MUSIC)

(A single candle is lit, perhaps next to a vessel of water and a branch that is starting to bud. "A Prayer at Candlemas" is recited or spoken around a circle by stanzas:)

A PRAYER AT CANDLEMAS

O difficult season
of brown and frost and fog,
of sudden snows and
days deep with grey
hanging heavy from heaven,
You are a difficult teacher.

Yes, buds swell on bushes.

Yes, some green survives
 winter freezes.
Yes, there is beauty somewhere
in the landscape
 of skeletal trees,
leaves rotting under snow,
turning into earth,
stones, holding their own,
moving slowly as
 Earth dances.

But I am weary of this time
where you ask me to
wait and look and love
the gradual growth of things
hidden from eyes
attuned to Yuletide lights
and the flash of
 holiday madness.

It is hard to embrace
quiet, near imperceptible changes,
while every day I'm made
 mindful of how fast
calendar sands
are running past me.

Slow me down.
Give me eyes attuned
to a winter-waiting palette
and miracles of red
 buds on branches,
strong against
 the pre-spring storms,
holding fast,
ready to burst again
impossibly
into blossom and green.

Give me inward eyes
for things almost hidden,
bud-like and brave in me.

Grant me a winter strength
to stand steady
when heavy snow
breaks what's brittle,
bends what's supple
in February bleak
 and hard March.

Open my soul
to the lengthening of light
and let me fall in love
 with the sun again,
rising from its low place
 in the sky,
arching toward spring
and a birth I have not
yet dreamed of.

FOR REFLECTION (WRITING TIME)

What is moving, quickening
within me these days?

Where do I feel glimmers of
new light, new life?

What obstacles are within me
that need "thawing" so that
spring might move inside of me?

What help do I need for the
renewal of my spirit, soul, life,
intentions, work?

*(OPTION FOR SHARING
OR SITTING IN THE QUIET)*

DISTRIBUTION OF CANDLES

(Each participant is given [or goes to a basket to get] a new, unlit candle [preferably one that contains some beeswax in its composition]. An explanation is given for the Candlemas tradition of blessing lights for use in prayer and worship.)

OPTION FOR BLESSING OF CANDLES

God Most High, Creator of All,
who summoned light into being
 in the day of our Beginning,
we bless You for both light
 and darkness,
for things seen and unseen.

We praise You for the gift
 of Jesus, Your Son,
who is light for us,
 and who has conquered
 the darkness of death.

Bless these candles,
 and all lights used in our
 dwellings and holy places
for our worship, reflection,
 and prayer in the year to come.

Winter into Spring

May they be for us gentle
   reminders of Your warmth
      and illumination
always present through
   the Spirit of Jesus,
in whose name we pray.

Amen.

LIGHTING OF CANDLES

(Each participant lights his/her candle from the single candle lit at the beginning of the service. Appropriate music is played and/or sung. People stand in a circle at the closing, and the following is prayed by a leader, by all together, or in sequence by individuals around the circle:)

CLOSING PRAYER

Living God,
source of all light,
bringer of new life
   and new seasons,
sustainer of all You have made:
Look upon us and upon
   all the Earth,
which is struggling
   in a long winter
of polar extremes, frozen by fear,
and broken apart
   by our divisions
of thought, belief, and practice.

Help us to see with new light,
to regard one another
   not as enemies,
but as members of a family
that You love more dearly than
a mother loves the children
born of her own womb.

As our outer world moves
   toward spring
      in this hemisphere,
make our hearts, souls,
   and minds
move to a new spring
of generosity, tolerance,
understanding, and compassion.

Stir up new life within us,
and move the obstacles
that inhibit us
from moving forward together,
especially the obstacles
we have created ourselves
because we forget
Who we are
and
Whose we are.

Restore us
and lead us
to a glorious spring.

Amen.

■ ■ ■

A Bouquet of Valentine Prayers

APPLICATION

Time before Saint Valentine's Day. The prayers below can be used separately or be gathered with music as a prayer service. They could also be used in conjunction with a reconciliation or healing service as preparations for a ritual that focuses on ways we have missed the mark in loving.

SET UP

If prayed privately, a lit candle may assist the meditation, especially if prayed before dawn or at evening. Any one or all of these prayers could be used as a way to center one's self for writing a Valentine greeting; or the prayers could be used within a Valentine greeting itself.

CALL TO PRAYER

If used within a service, a simple explanation might be given about the background of Saint Valentine, the day named after him, and the practice of sending written signs of love. Prayer could begin with a call to mindfulness (quiet, intentional breathing or meditational music or a song). The prayer might close with the sharing of chocolate!

A Meditation

At the Feast of Saint Valentine

O Power of Love,
Sustainer of All That Is,
Living Force of the Universe,

I give thanks this day
for those whose love
has brought me into being
—my ancestors, my people,
my parents;

    (I pause and remember.)

for those whose love has shaped
my journey—my relatives,
my teachers, my influences;

    (I pause and remember.)

and for those whose affection
and care sustain me this day—
my friends, my colleagues,
my family.

    (I pause and remember.)

I acknowledge this day that I am
connected to Loving Mystery
beyond my comprehension,
that my care for this planet is
a necessary act of mindfulness
and appreciation, and that I am
nourished and enlivened by
giving and receiving affection.

    (I pause and remember.)

I also acknowledge
that my love matters:
    loving people is
        a good vocation;
attending to my emotional
health and physical well-being is
appropriate and needed;
surrendering to love
    takes practice and time.

    *(I pause and recall my
    various efforts to be loving
    in my words and deeds.)*

I ask Your help this day,
that I may be a more abundant
reflection of Love:
that my words may be kinder
to others,
    especially to those
        who tax my patience;
that my actions be more
gracious to the human family,
    especially to those whose
        lives are especially in need
        of any signs of human
        attention;

(I pause and remember those in need.)

that my thoughts be more
care-full and compassionate,
    especially of those whom
        I tend to shut out or
        whom I make my enemy.

    *(I pause and imagine the
    opportunities of this day.)*

Make me mindful this day
of the signs of Love that are
all around me:
    of good words spoken,
    of gentle touch extended,
    of important things that
        spring from appreciation
        and true passion,
    of deeds that are born
        of generosity and of
        real understanding.

    *(I pause and open my heart
    to being loved.)*

Grant me the power this day
    to live with thoughtful
        intention
    in my speech, choices,
        and actions,
    so that I may build the habit
        of living gracefully
        and with love
    for the people and
        experiences that shape
        my life,
    which is Your gift of Love
        to me each day.

    *(I pause and breathe in
    this prayer.)*

AMEN.

■ ■ ■

A Litany

For a Valentine Prayer Service

This litany can be read straight through, or time can be added after each statement for deeper remembrance and reflection. Parts in bold type are read by all.

O Great Creator Spirit, You hold us always in Your care. We make our life journey with You and in the company of others who share wisdom and experience with us. We now call to mind the people who have shaped us into the people we are today:

For those who from our early years have been models of loving:

> **We give thanks and remember.**

For those who have been our teachers in life, who have strengthened our self-esteem:

> **We give thanks and remember.**

For those who have shared the gift of friendship and led us to self knowledge:

> **We give thanks and remember.**

For those who have shared our love, and for those who endured our rejections and loved us still:

> **We give thanks and remember.**

For the people who have taught us compassion, mercy, forgiveness, and true strength:

> **We give thanks and remember.**

For the ways we have learned valuable lessons in the loss of love, the challenges of love, and the end of love:

> **We give thanks and remember.**

For the ways we have deepened in our capacity to love and in our understanding:

> **We give thanks and remember.**

For the people we love now, and for the people to love in the years to come:

> **We give thanks and remember.**

Gracious God, the tendrils of love that others offer sometimes feel frayed and damaged.

The love I have to share with others sometimes feels shallow, strained, or contrived.

The love that comes from You sometimes feels distant and unreal.

When love is less than I would like it to be, give me the patience to quiet my heart long enough to bring it to the edge of Your embrace. There, may I find the place where You can touch my fragmented heart and bring it closer to being whole.

I ask this for the sake of Your love.

Amen.

∎ ∎ ∎

A Prayer

Before Writing a Valentine Card

O Holy One,
You who are to be found
in small gestures
as well as great miracles,
Grant Your quiet grace
to my words and my intentions
as I remember the person
who will receive the card
that I write today.

You know the human heart.
You perceive our needs,
our hopes, our hurts,
our deepest longings.
You know how well we weather
    seasons of celebration
        or times of isolation.

Grant that my words touch
the spirit of the one
    to whom I write
with
Kindness, Mirth,
Gentleness, Care,
Good Memory, Love,
or Tenderness.

Grant my phrases
generosity and genuine regard
as I reach out in
    this simple gesture.

If possible or if needed,
may this card serve as a
restored or renewed bridge,
an outstretched hand,
or as a sign of forgiveness
    or acceptance.

Travel with this Valentine token
and let it do a simple good work
in the life of the one who
receives it.

Amen.

■ ■ ■

Galileo's Birthday

February 15   Dedicated to Sr. Eileen Currie, MSC

BACKGROUND

Along with making improvements to the telescope and contributing many other inventions and scientific insights, Galileo Galilei (February 15, 1564–January 8, 1642) embraced heliocentrism (the sun-centered reality of our solar system) and bolstered the empirical data that led to this conclusion. This position put him in great disfavor with the (geocentric) Church. He was tried for heresy and placed under house arrest for the remainder of his life. For some he is a kind of patron spirit, representing the courage and tenacity to hold fast to what is true despite formidable opinion to the contrary.

"The Bible shows the way to go to heaven, not the way the heavens go."
GALILEO

For some time, Gentle God,
it has seemed those heavens that
   I know
are out of synch with a more
   popularly
   and heavily held view
of the universe (as we don't
   know it).

I cannot fully explain how
   the scope I use
tells the position of my rightful
   center
though I am certain
that were I able to reveal my
   ways and
explanations that make sense
   to me,
I would only be belittled
   and ridiculed
   and locked away.

And so the forces of discord
   rise up.
I feel the weight of a mighty
   censure,
the constant burn of many
   angry words,
and the vitriolic explosion
   that accompanies
so much well-defended
   contrariness.

Most High, Most True,
   Long-Suffering God,
send me the courage
   of father Galileo,
that I might hold fast to what
   is true,
and keep my eyes on the plumb
   line
that runs its trustable course
between Thy heavens
   and my heart.

"Though my soul may set in darkness, it will rise in perfect light; I have loved the stars too fondly to be fearful of the night."
ATTRIBUTED TO GALILEO

∎ ∎ ∎

Presidents Day

A Prayer for Those in Civic Leadership

God Most High,
font of wisdom and compassion,
source of true authority
in heaven and on earth,

We ask Your blessing
upon all those who
    have been selected
for leadership in our country,
    most especially for
    our president,
the cabinet, and the president's
    advisors.

We humbly beseech You
to pour out Your Spirit
on those whose task it is
to manage resources,
    to make laws,
and to lead and inspire
    the people,
especially in
    these difficult times.

We ask that they may do
    what they can do
to bind up the wounds
    of our nation
and to raise up those who are
    heavily burdened
    by economic and
    social realities.

We ask that they be inspired
    by the life of Your Son,
    who sought not to be exalted
to high earthly status,
but to serve,
especially to serve those
    who were ignored
    and cast out by others.

Heal the divisions of this nation.
Give us the courage
    and the grace
to work with one another,
no matter our politics,
    our creeds,
or our seeming differences,
so that those who are homeless,
    and naked,
and hungry, and forgotten,
may find in our individual
    actions
and in our collective will
the desire to make known
Your Reign of justice and mercy.

We ask all this in the name
    of Jesus,
Our Lord and Brother,
forever and ever.

Amen.

▪ ▪ ▪

In The Endless Winter

A Prayer and Reflection for Survival

Spirit, Maker, Holy One,
    Turner of the Endless Seasons,
Save me from these swollen
    clouds, grey and pregnant
    with cold rage!
I cannot bear another onslaught.
I am unready for another inch
    of snow, or slush, or rain.

The unrelenting cold
    has taken me prisoner;
    I ache in every bone.
My nose drips as much
    as any eave of my house.
I despair of the smell
    of wool around my face,
and these layers of fiber,
    feather, and flannel
    are crusting into
    a walking tomb.

There is no buoyant holiday
    to distract me from
    this stretch of days
that keep me confined,
    or keep me captive
    in a car iced and sliding
    out of control
in city streets that compound
    the steely tones of
    JanuFebruMarcharary.

Flame down! Flame Down!
    Oh warm Harbinger!
Cradle me still when mercury
    falls with a heavier,
    harder night,
on the brown, bare days
    that hang overlong
    on heart, head.

Sacred Flowerbed,
    release your secret
    under-earthed;
grant me a slip of a dream
    of green, a glimpse
    of snow drop, crocus,
    even weeds.

Sing, Mother Over Ages,
    into the pummeled,
    silent, secret soil,
that star-touched song of life
    emerging out of madness,
our winter madness,
    made more wild
    by months inside,
warmed only by vacant TV glow,
    and taunting masquerades
    of island escapes.

From Earth's leaf-lined tombs
    let rise the child's voice
    and the child's hope,
and summon me
    out of my battered, bruised,
    and frosty shell
into a warmer dance,
    free of cold curses
    and ready for Spring.

FOR REFLECTION (WRITTEN OR SHARED)

- What lessons does winter teach me? What am I being taught today?

- What lessons am I open to? What do I dread?

- What lessons am I reluctant to receive?

- What of winter leads me to hope? To deeper mystery?

- What of winter can I receive with gratitude?

■ ■ ■

Past Epiphany

Let's Get Ordinary/The Sacredness of All Days

BACKGROUND

Ordinary Time refers to a season of the liturgical Churches (Catholic, Anglican, Lutheran, and some others) that is not Advent/Christmas/Epiphany or Lent/Easter/Pentecost. Ordinary Time is celebrated in two segments and comprises the largest part of the liturgical calendar. The weeks (beginning on Sundays) of Ordinary Time are numbered, and some of those weeks include special solemnities or feasts. The word "ordinary" is not meant to indicate "insignificant" but more a sense of "ordered" or "counted," that all time represents the movement to the fullness of the Reign of God, and, thus, all time is considered sacred. The Church color for Ordinary Time is green, indicating growth and vitality.

APPLICATION

This prayer can be used at the outset of Ordinary Time, per se, or can be used as a prayer for a community (parts can be divided for separate readers or "all"), or individuals (change the pronouns) to begin a day. A breath between each stanza is advised.

The root of the prayer is that all time is gift, is sacred, is full of the Divine Possible. So much rests on our ability to be open to what is.

God of Many Names,
of all seasons and all times,
This day,
this moment in our journey,
we greet You.

We know that You
    are here with us,
And we are happy
to be here with You.

There is nothing better
than the blessing of this NOW.

Our breath, our being,
our imagination and reason
are rooted in You.

Our future, our possibilities,
our best dreams and our hopes
come from Your hands.

Gather us into Your care
and open us to the gift
    of this day,
and to the gift of all days
    to come.

Guide us by Your Great Spirit
and lead us to those places
    Where You are—

hidden in human faces,
speaking in human need,
waiting in human flesh,
ready to be known anew.

Feed us with what
    vwe really need—

with beauty and grace,

with a word that endures,

with love enough,

and life enough.

Grant us generous hearts,

Teach us kindness for our selves,

Show us compassion for others,

And grant us gratitude
for all that You pour out
    in our lives
every day,

That we may live
    into the fullness of
that place where You are
completely Your self
beyond all time

and where we,
at last,
can be completely at Home.

AMEN.

■ ■ ■

At Mardi Gras

A Prayer Before the Masks I Wear

Most High God,
You who know
    my inmost being,
my every flaw,
my shining beauty,
my blatant darknesses,
and my hidden lights:

Once again
it is the appointed
festival of excesses:
of booze and foods,
flung beads,
grotesque behaviors,
and convenient costumes
to hide every impropriety.

So
once again,
in keeping with the season,
I don the mask I place
between me and You,
between me and the world,
between me and my
    conscious self.

You see how carefully I cradle it;
how knowingly I attach its
ribbons and cords
so it will fit just right
against the face
that is
to me
just a little too tired,
too dull,
too not-damn-fabulous
to be worn into
    the carnival world
(there are expectations after all).

Sigh if You must,
but You must know
how these masks
have their purposes:

Sometimes I wear the mask
to reveal a part of me
    that is hidden,
but still a real part of me.

Sometimes I wear
    the mask for protection
because a part of me is
too fragile
and the world is
too harsh
against me.

Sometimes I wear the mask
because it is easier to
adopt the
Image
rather than to
live the
reality
of all of who I am.

Help me to know
when it is time to
strip away the masks I wear.

When the Mardi Gras garbage
has been
gathered away at midnight,
grant me the grace to walk
in the dawn of honesty,
to experience
Your acceptance of me
As I Am,
Unadorned,
Flaws shining,
Flash cast away,
My face
Open to the world,
Because it is radiant and brave
With Your beholding of me
And loving me
As I am.

Amen.